ANTHONY DOERR was born and raised in Cleveland, Ohio. He is the author of the story collections *The Shell Collector* and *Memory Wall*, and the novels *About Grace* and *All the Light We Cannot See*, which was awarded the 2015 Pulitzer Prize for Fiction and the 2015 Andrew Carnegie Medal for Excellence in Fiction. Doerr's short stories have won the 2010 Story Prize, which is considered the most prestigious prize in the U.S. for a collection of short stories, and the *Sunday Times* EFG Short Story Award, which is the largest prize in the world for a single short story. His work has been translated into over forty languages. Doerr lives in Boise, Idaho with his wife and two sons.

Praise for *Four Seasons in Rome*:

'Doerr is dazzling in this book, in the way he celebrates the joys as well as the pain of being a parent and in love, being a writer and being in Rome, reminding us that certain experiences never grow stale when they are expressed through the fresh eyes of a real writer'

AZAR NAFISI, author of *Reading Lolita in Tehran*

'A funny, precise, touching account of cultural barricades crossed and fatherly exhaustions overcome; a story of the universalities of parenting and the specificities of Roman life' ADAM GOPNIK, author of *Through the Children's Gate* and *From Paris to the Moon*

'A love letter written with the ear of a musician, the sensibility of a Buddha, the heart of an inamorato. Rome is the chosen beloved, but Doerr's true subject is writing'

SANDRA CISNEROS, author of *Caramelo*

'That Doerr sees so acutely in our "astoundingly, intricately, breathtaking beautiful world" makes it all the more happy a thing that he creates, on the printed page, beauty of his own' *Bookslut*

Also by Anthony Doerr

All the Light We Cannot See
Memory Wall
About Grace
The Shell Collector

FOUR SEASONS IN ROME

*On Twins, Insomnia and the Biggest
Funeral in the History of the World*

ANTHONY DOERR

4th ESTATE • London

4th Estate
An imprint of HarperCollins*Publishers*
1 London Bridge Street
London SE1 9GF
www.4thEstate.co.uk

Originally published in the United States in 2007 by Scribner
First published in Great Britain in 2008 by 4th Estate

This edition published by 4th Estate in 2016

7

A catalogue record for this book
is available from the British Library

ISBN 978-0-00-726529-9

Printed and bound by
CPI Group (UK) Ltd, Croydon, CR0 4YY

MIX
Paper from
responsible sources
FSC™ C007454

FSC™ is a non-profit international organisation established to promote
the responsible management of the world's forests. Products carrying the
FSC label are independently certified to assure consumers that they come
from forests that are managed to meet the social, economic and
ecological needs of present and future generations,
and other controlled sources.

Find out more about HarperCollins and the environment at
www.harpercollins.co.uk/green

for Henry and Owen

Rain falls, clouds rise, rivers dry up, hailstorms sweep down; rays scorch, and impinging from every side on the earth in the middle of the world, then are broken and recoil and carry with them the moisture they have drunk up. Steam falls from on high and again returns on high. Empty winds sweep down, and then go back again with their plunder. So many living creatures draw their breath from the upper air; but the air strives in the opposite direction, and the earth pours back breath to the sky as if to a vacuum. Thus as nature swings to and fro like a kind of sling, discord is kindled by the velocity of the world's motion.

PLINY THE ELDER, FROM THE
Natural History, AD 77

FALL

ITALY LOOMS. WE MAKE CHECKLISTS — DIAPERS, CRIB bedding, a book light. Baby formula. Two dozen Nutri-Grain bars. We have never eaten Nutri-Grain bars in our lives, but now, suddenly, it seems important to have some.

I stare at our new Italian-to-English pocket dictionary and worry. Is "Here is my passport" in there? Is "Where for God's sake can I buy some baby wipes?"

We pretend to be calm. Neither of us is willing to consider that tomorrow we'll pile onto an Airbus with six-month-old twins and climb to thirty-seven thousand feet and stay there for fourteen hours. Instead we zip and unzip our duffels, take the wheels off the stroller, and study small, grainy photos of St. Peter's on ricksteves.com.

Rain in Boise; wind in Denver. The airplane hurtles through the troposphere at six hundred miles per hour. Owen sleeps in a mound of blankets between our feet. Henry sleeps in my arms. All the way across the Atlantic, there is turbulence; bulkheads shake, glasses tinkle, galley latches open and close.

We are moving from Boise, Idaho, to Rome, Italy, a

place I've never been. When I think of Italy, I imagine decadence, dark brown oil paintings, emperors in sandals. I see a cross-section of a school-project Colosseum, fashioned from glue and sugar cubes; I see a navy-blue-and-white soap dish, bought in Florence, chipped on one corner, that my mother kept beside her bathroom sink for thirty years.

More clearly than anything else, I see a coloring book I once got for Christmas entitled *Ancient Rome*. Two babies slurped milk from the udders of a wolf. A Caesar grinned in his leafy crown. A slinky, big-pupiled maiden posed with a jug beside a fountain. Whatever Rome was to me then—seven years old, Christmas night, snowflakes dashing against the windows, a lighted spruce blinking on and off downstairs, crayons strewn across the carpet—it's hardly clearer now: outlines of elephants and gladiators, cartoonish palaces in the backgrounds, a sense that I had chosen all the wrong colors, aquamarine for chariots, goldenrod for skies.

On the television screen planted in the seat-back in front of me, our little airplane icon streaks past Marseilles, Nice. A bottle of baby formula, lying sideways in the seat pocket, soaks through the fabric and drips onto my carry-on, but I don't reach down to straighten it for fear I will wake Henry. We have crossed from North America to Europe in the time it takes to show a Lindsay Lohan movie and two episodes of *Everybody Loves Raymond*. The outside temperature is minus sixty degrees Fahrenheit.

A taxi drops us in front of a palace: stucco and travertine, a five-bay façade, a staircase framed by topiaries. The gatekeeper stubs his cigarette on a shoe sole and says, in English, "You're the ones with the twins?" He shakes our hands, gives us a set of keys.

Our apartment is in a building next to the palace. The front gate is nine feet tall and iron and scratched in a thousand places; it looks as if wild dogs have been trying to break into the courtyard. A key unlocks it; we find the entrance around the side. The boys stare up from their car seats with huge eyes. We load them into a cage elevator with wooden doors that swing inward. Two floors rattle past. I hear finches, truck brakes. Neighbors clomp through the stairwell; a door slams. There are the voices of children. The gate, three stories down, clangs hugely.

Our door opens into a narrow hallway. I fill it slowly with bags. Shauna, my wife, carries the babies inside. The apartment is larger than we could have hoped: two bedrooms, two bathrooms, new cabinets, twelve-foot ceilings, tile floors that carry noise. There's an old desk, a navy blue couch. The refrigerator is hidden inside a cupboard. There's a single piece of art: a poster of seven or eight gondolas crossing a harbor, a hazy piazza in the background.

The apartment's jewel is a terrace, which we reach through a narrow door in the corner of the kitchen, as if the architect recognized the need for a doorway only at the last moment. It squats over the building's entrance, thirty feet across, fifty feet up. From it we can look between treetops at jigsaw pieces of Rome: terra-cotta roofs, three or four domes, a double-decker campanile, the scattered green of terrace gardens, everything hazed and strange and impossible.

The air is moist and warm. If anything, it smells vaguely of cabbage.

"This is ours?" Shauna asks. "The whole terrace?" It is. Except for our door, there is no other entrance onto it.

We lower the babies into mismatched cribs that don't look especially safe. A mosquito floats through the kitchen. We share a Nutri-Grain bar. We eat five packages of saltines. We have moved to Italy.

For a year I'll be a fellow at the American Academy in Rome. There are no students here, no faculty, only a handful of artists and scholars, each of whom is given a year in Rome to pursue independent projects.

I'm a fellow in literature. All I have to do is write. I don't even have to show anyone what I write. In return, they give me a studio, the keys to this apartment, two bath mats, a stack of bleached towels every Thursday, and $1,300 a month. We'll live on the Janiculum Hill, a green wave of trees and villas that rears a few hundred yards and a series of centuries-old stone staircases above the Roman neighborhood called Trastevere.

I stand on a chair on the terrace and try to find the Tiber River in the maze of distant buildings but see no boats, no bridges. A guidebook at the Boise Public Library said Trastevere was charming, crammed with pre-Renaissance churches, medieval lanes, nightclubs. All I see is haze: rooftops, treetops. I hear the murmur of traffic.

A palm tree out the window traps the sunset. The kitchen faucet drips. We did not apply for this fellowship; we did not even know that it existed. Nine months ago we got a letter from the American Academy of Arts and

Letters saying my work had been nominated by an anonymous committee. Four months later we got a letter saying we had won. Shauna was still in the hospital, our sons twelve hours old, when I stood in front of our apartment in the slush and found the envelope in the mail.

Our toilet has two buttons to flush it, one twice the size of the other. We discuss: I contend they produce the same amount of water; Shauna says the bigger button is for bigger jobs.

As it always is with leaving home, it is the details that displace us. The windows have no screens. Sirens, passing in the street, are a note lower. So is the dial tone on our red plastic telephone. When we pee, our pee lands not in water but on porcelain.

The bathroom faucets read *C* and *F* and the *C* is for *calda,* not cold but hot. The refrigerator is the size of a beer cooler. An unlabeled steel lever protrudes from the wall above the cooktop. For gas? Hot water?

The cribs the Academy has loaned us have no bumpers or sheets but do have what we decide must be pillows: inch-high rectangles of foam, sheathed in cotton.

The dishwashing soap smells like salted limes. The mosquitoes are bigger. Instead of closets, the bedrooms have big, musty wardrobes.

Shauna rummages through the triangular space that is to become our kitchen, dining room, and living room. "There's no oven."

"No oven?"

"No oven."

"Maybe Italians don't use ovens?"

She gives me a look. "They invented pizza."

Fifteen minutes before midnight, the digital clock on the microwave reads 23:45. What will midnight be? 0:00?

That first night we go to sleep around midnight, but the boys are awake at one, crying in their strange cribs. Shauna and I pass each other in the hall, each rocking a baby.

Jet lag is a dryness in the eyes, a loose wire in the spine. Wake up in Boise, go to bed in Rome. The city is a field of shadows beyond the terrace railing. The bones of Keats and Raphael and St. Peter molder somewhere out there. The pope dreams a half mile away. Owen blinks up at me, mouth open, a crease in his forehead, as though his soul is still somewhere over the Atlantic, trying to catch up with the rest of him.

By the time the apartment is light again, none of us have slept. We need money, we need food. I reassemble our stroller and wrestle it down the stairwell. Shauna straps in the boys. Beyond the front gate the sidewalk stretches right and left. The sky is broken and humid; a little car rifles past and sets a plastic bag spinning in its wake.

"There's more traffic to the left," Shauna says.

"Is that good?"

"Maybe more traffic means more stores?"

I am resisting this logic when a neighbor appears behind us. Small, freckled, powerful-looking. She is American. Her name is Laura. Her husband is a fellow at the Academy in landscape architecture. She has just put her children on the bus for school and is now carrying out her recycling and going to buy ground beef.

She leads us left. Fifty feet up the sidewalk, four streets

converge beneath a blocky stucco archway called the Porta San Pancrazio, a gate in Rome's old defensive walls. There are no stoplights. Little cars push forward, each looking for a gap. A city bus heaves into the mix. Then a flatbed stacked with furniture. Then a pair of motor scooters. Everyone appears to be inching toward the same alley, where, as soon as they're free of the logjam, the vehicles streak away, charging between lines of parked cars, their side mirrors either tucked in or torn off.

Laura chats all the way. As if today were just another day, as if our lives were not in peril, as if Rome were Cincinnati. Are there even crosswalks? Horns blare. A taxi nearly shaves off the stroller's front wheels. "What airline did you guys fly?" Laura yells. Shauna says, "My goodness." I feel like crouching in the gutter with my babies in my arms.

Another scooter (a *motorino,* Laura tells us) squeezes into the melee. The driver braces a four-foot banana plant in a pot on the little riding platform between his shoes. Its leaves flap against his shoulders as he passes.

Laura marches across the intersection, flings her recycling into a series of bins, points out storefronts farther down the street. She seems impossibly comfortable; she is an island of composure. I worry: Can we talk so loudly? In English?

The boys don't make a sound. It's hot. Apartment buildings loom above shops, hundreds of balconies crammed with geraniums, pygmy palms, tomatoes. Outside bars, teenagers drink coffee from glasses. Men in blue jumpsuits and combat boots stand in front of banks, handguns strapped to their hips. We pass a Fiat dealership in a storefront no bigger than the beauty salon next to it. We pass a pizzeria; an old man behind the glass counter plucks a flower off the end of a zucchini.

In the baby food section of a *farmacia* I hunt for anything recognizable and find labels illustrated with rabbits, sheep, and—worse—ponies.

"In Italy," Laura says, "My Pretty Pony is a snack."

She helps us find an ATM; she shows us where to buy disposable diapers. She sets us straight on the names of the neighborhoods: "Trastevere is behind us, down the stairs. The Janiculum, where we live, is just the name of the hill. Our neighborhood, the one we're walking in, is called Monteverde."

"Monteverde," I say, practicing. Green hill. Before Laura leaves, she points us toward the vegetable market. *"A presto,"* she says, which leaves me reaching for my phrase book. *Prestare?* To give?

Then she's gone. I think of Dante in Purgatory, turning to tell Virgil something, only to find Virgil is no longer there.

At the produce stand—we learn the hard way—you're not supposed to touch the vegetables; you point at the *insalatine* or *pomodori* and the merchant will set them on the scale. The butcher's eggs sit in open cartons, roasting in the sun. There are no tags on any of his meat; I gesture at something pink and boneless and cross my fingers.

The Kit Kats are packaged not in orange labels but in red. They taste better. So do the pears. We devour one and bleed pear juice all over the canopy of the stroller. The tomatoes—a dozen of them in a paper bag—appear to give off light.

The babies suck on biscuits. We glide through sun and shadow.

Two blocks from the market, on a street called Quat-
tro Venti—the Four Winds—the smell of a bakery
blows onto the sidewalk. I lock the stroller brake, pull
open the door, and step into a throng. Everyone jostles
everyone else; people who have just entered stoop and
dive and squirm toward the counter. Should I be taking
a number? Do I shout my order? I try to run through my
Italian vocabulary: eight afternoons at a Berlitz in Boise,
$400, and right now all I can remember is *tazza da tè*.
Teacup.

A woman with whiskers is pressed against me, my
chin in her hair. She smells like old milk. Loaves shuttle
back and forth over my head. I know *ciabatta*. I know
focaccia.

Behind the counter the only Italians I have seen wearing shorts slide about on the flour-slick tile in white sneakers. The crowd has driven me into a corner. Men who
have just entered are getting their orders taken, passing
bills forward.

Poppy seeds, sesame seeds, a crumpled wad of wax
paper. I am a kernel beneath the millstone. Through the
glass doors I can see Shauna crouched over the boys, who
are screaming. Everything swims. What are the words?
Scusi? Permesso? We can live without bread. All year if we
have to. I lower my head and grapple my way out.

The bakery is not my only failure. In a hardware store
I look around for key rings, but the owner stands in front
of me with his hands clasped together, eager to help, and
I don't know how to say "key ring" or "I'm just looking,"
so for a minute we face each other, wordless.

"Luce per notte," I finally arrive at. *"Per bambini."* And
although I'm not there to buy children's night-lights, he

shows me one, so I buy it. The key rings wait until I can
return with a dictionary.

According to a two-sentence project summary I had to
send the Academy, I've come to Rome to continue writing
my third book, a second novel, this one about the German
occupation of a village in Normandy between 1940 and
1944. I have brought maybe fifty pages of prose, some
photos of B-17s dropping firebombs, and a mess of scribbled notes.

My writing studio is in the palace next door to our
apartment building: the American Academy itself, hushed,
gigantic, imposing. While the babies nap, that first full
afternoon in Rome, I pass through the big gate, wave to the
gatekeeper in his little shed, and carry my notebooks up the
front stairs. An arrow to the left points to "office"; an arrow
to the right points to "library." The courtyard is full of
gravel and jasmine. A fountain trickles. I nod to a man in
a black T-shirt with bloodshot eyes, his forearms smeared
with oil paint.

Studio 235 is a rectangle with high ceilings called the
Tom Andrews Studio, after a hemophilic poet who held
the same fellowship I now have. He worked here in 2000;
he died in 2002. His studio contains two desks, a little cot,
and an office chair with the stuffing torn out of it.

Tom Andrews, I heard once, broke a world record by
clapping his hands continuously for fourteen hours and
thirty-one minutes. The first line of his second book is
"May the Lord Jesus Christ bless the hemophiliac's
motorcycle."

I talk to him as I slide furniture around.

"Tom," I say, "I've been in Italy twenty hours and I've been asleep for one of them."

"Tom," I say, "I'm putting three books on your shelves."

The window in the Tom Andrews Studio is six or seven feet high, and looks out at the three acres of trees and lawns behind the Academy. Bisecting the view, maybe twelve feet beyond the sill, is the trunk of a magnificent Italian pine.

All over the neighborhood I've noticed these trees: soaring, branchless trunks; high, subdividing crowns like the heads of neurons. In the months to come I will hear them called Italian pines, Roman pines, Mediterranean pines, stone pines, parasol pines, and umbrella pines—all the same thing: *Pinus pinea*. Regal trees, astounding trees, trees both unruly and composed at once, like princes who sleep stock-still but dream swarming dreams.

A half dozen umbrella pines stand behind the embassy across the street; a line of them thrust their heads over the 360-year-old wall that borders the Academy's lawns. I never expected Rome to have trees like these, for a city of 3 million people to be a living garden, moss in the sidewalk cracks, streamers of ivy sashaying in archways, ancient walls wearing a haze of capers, thyme sprouting from church steeples. This morning the cobblestones were slick with algae. In the streets Laura escorted us through, clandestine stands of bamboo rustled in apartment courtyards; pines stood next to palms, cypress next to orange trees; I saw a thatch of mint growing from a sidewalk crack outside a video store.

Of the three books I've brought, one is about the Nazi occupation of France, because of the novel I'm trying to write. One is a selection of excerpts from Pliny the Elder's

Natural History, because the jacket copy says it offers a view of the natural world as it was understood in first-century Rome. The last is a field guide to trees. The tree book gives the umbrella pine a half of a page. *The bark is gray-brown and fissured; the scales fall off from time to time, leaving light brown patches.*

A spreading walnut, a grove of olives; lindens, crab apples, a hedge made entirely of rosemary. The walls that hem in these gardens rise thirty feet in places, the stone-work bleached by time, the upper reaches punctuated with crossbow loops, the ramparts bristling with weeds. Before electricity, before the umbrella pine out the window was even a pinecone, when the night sky above the Janiculum was as awash with stars as any sky anywhere, Galileo Galilei assembled his new telescope at a banquet in this very garden, just beneath my window, and showed guests the heavens.

Fifty yards away, in our apartment, Shauna grapples with the babies. I think of Owen's swiveling head, Henry's circular eyes. "They are miracles," I tell the ghost of Tom Andrews. Born from cells smaller than the period at the end of this sentence—*much* smaller than that period—the boys are suddenly big and loud and soak the fronts of their shirts with drool.

I open a notebook to an empty page. I try to put down a few sentences about gratitude, about wonder.

We fry pork chops in a dented skillet, drink wine from water glasses. Chimney swifts race across the terrace. All night the boys wake and cry in their strange cribs. I feed Henry at 12:40 a.m. (the microwave clock reads 0:40) and swaddle him and finally convince him to fall asleep. Then I lie down on the sofa with my head on a stack of diapers and two spit-up cloths stretched over my body like napkins; our only blanket is on the bed, on top of Shauna. Ten minutes. Twenty minutes. Why even bother? It's only a dream before Owen will wake.

What did Columbus write in his log as he set out from Spain? "Above all, it is fitting that I forget about sleeping and devote much attention to navigation in order to accomplish this."

Henry wakes again at two. Owen is up at three. Each time, rising out of a half sleep, it takes a full minute to remember what I have forgotten: I am a father; we have moved to Italy.

All night I carry one crying baby or the other onto the terrace. The air is warm and sweet. Stars burn here and there. In the distance little strands of glitter climb the hills.

"Molto, molto bella," our taxi driver, Roberto, told us as he drove us, our seven duffel bags, and our forty-five-pound stroller here from the airport. He had a scrubby chin and two cell phones and cringed whenever the babies made a noise.

"Non c'è una città più bella di Roma," he said. There is no city more beautiful than Rome.

On our second morning in Italy we push the stroller out the front gate and turn right. The boys moan; the axles rattle. Little cars shoot past. We round a corner and a chain-link fence gives way to hedges, which give way to the side of a monumental marble-and-granite fountain. We wheel gape-jawed around to its front.

Five niches in a six-columned headboard as big as a house unload water into a shallow, semicircular pool. Seven lines of Latin swarm across its face; griffins and eagles ride its capitals. The Romans, we'll learn later, call it simply *il Fontanone*. The big fountain. It was completed in 1690; it had taken seventy-eight years to build. The travertine seems almost to glow; it is as if lights have been implanted inside the stone.

Across the street is another marvel: a railing, some benches, and a perch with a view over the entire city. We dodge traffic, roll the boys to the parapet. Here is all of Rome: ten thousand rooftops, church domes, bell towers, palaces, apartments; an airplane traversing slowly from right to left; the city extending back across the plain. Strings of distant towns marble hills at the horizon. Beneath us, for as far as we can see, drifts a bluish haze— it is as if the city were submerged beneath a lake, and a wind were ruffling its surface.

"This," Shauna says, whispering, "is fifty yards from our front door."

The fountain roars at our backs. The city swirls below us.

Farther down the street is a church, a little piazza, and the top of a twisting ramp of staircases. The steps are worn and greasy; dried leaves rustle on the sloped landings between. I take the front of the stroller; Shauna takes the back.

She asks, "Are you ready?"

"I think so. Are you?"

"I think so."

But who knows if we are? We start downward. The stroller weighs forty-five pounds; the boys each weigh about fifteen. With each step it seems to get heavier. There are maybe twenty stairs, then four or five connected ramps, then more stairs. Sweat drips from the tip of my nose. My palms slip. Any moment the stroller will tear free, start bouncing, gain momentum, hurtle around the corner, and explode in front of a bus.

We descend into the unknown. The ramps are lined with stations of the cross. Jesus gets his crown of thorns; Jesus collapses beneath the weight of the cross. Someone has set a bouquet of pink roses beside the twelfth station: *Into your hands I commend my spirit.*

At the bottom an archway opens onto a street buzzing with cars. Henry starts crying. We zigzag; we hold our breath and sprint. "Frogger!" Shauna says, halfway out of breath, and grins at me.

The traffic fades. We stick a pacifier between Henry's lips. Trastevere is full of medieval houses and clotheslines and drinking fountains that appear to be permanently turned on. Little cars are parked in impossible places. In front of one building maybe eighty scooters stand hand-grip to handgrip; there is the temptation to give one a kick to see if they'll all go down.

Julius Caesar lived in this neighborhood. So did Cleopatra. Every Roman we pass smiles at the boys. *Gemellini,* they say. Little twins. And something like *piccininni.* Or *porcellini?* Small pigs?

Grown men, in suits, stop and crouch over the stroller and croon. Older men in particular. *Che carini. Che belli.* What cuties. What beauties. The stroller could be loaded with braying zebras and it would not attract any more attention.

We get lost. Shauna changes a diaper on the cobblestones while I peer into a map. Is this Vicolo del Cinque? Piazza San Cosimato? In a pasta shop—a glass counter, piles of tortellini, yards of fettuccine—I manage to buy a kilogram of orange ravioli stuffed with pumpkin and ricotta, the pasta dusty with flour. *"I suoi bambini,"* the shopkeeper tells me, watching my eyes to see if I'm following. *"Sono belli."* Your babies, they are beautiful.

I carry the package into the street feeling victorious. A breeze seethes in some locust trees at the head of the alley and their little leaves fly past us, a blizzard of gold. Through a doorway I can see a dim kitchen, copper pans hanging against whitewash. A woman stares into a sink, ensconced in steam, her hair stacked in a complicated tower.

Sixty hours ago I was buying Pampers at an Albertsons supermarket in Boise. Now I stand near the ghost of what, two thousand years ago, was supposedly an amphitheater flooded regularly by the Emperor Augustus to stage mock naval battles. We stare at clothing shops, a bookstore, try to imagine the keel of an imperial trireme slicing past above us.

Shauna asks, "Shall we go home?" At first I think she means Idaho. But she's only gesturing behind us, where the spine of green that is the Janiculum arches above the rooftops. A river of leaves streams past our feet. Owen yawns against his stroller straps. Henry sucks his pacifier.

We race across a street whizzing with buses. We start back up the stairs. We see no fat people.

The twins are fraternal. Henry's hair is blond with a touch of white. His eyes are yellow-brown. His skin is pale, and a cleft divides his chin, and when he reaches for something, his eyes widen and his lips purse. He waves things back and forth—a plastic spoon, a fuzzy rattle—to see if they'll make a sound. When the air is humid, his hair fluffs high on his head and bright orange balls of wax appear in his ears.

Owen's hair is thicker, the color of varnished walnut. One minute he's inconsolable, the next he's eating homogenized pears by the jarful and grinning like a madman. He refuses to go to sleep. He wakes screaming at 3 a.m.; he wakes for good at 5 a.m.

Shauna and I have meandering, sleep-starved debates: Why won't Owen sleep? Gas? Jet lag? Italy? Having a baby is like bringing a noisy, inarticulate foreigner into your house and trying to guess what he likes to eat. With Owen we begin to believe we are missing something obvious, a splinter, a rash, an allergy, some affliction experienced parents would diagnose in a minute.

"You know what I think it is?" Shauna asks. "There's too much light coming through the bedroom window."

So ten minutes after the boys should be going to bed, on our fourth night in Rome, I tear apart diaper boxes and climb out on the sill in the second bathroom, fifty feet above the sidewalk, and tape ragged sheets of cardboard over all four panes. Shauna wheels Owen's crib down the hall, into the bathroom, and wedges it between the tub and sink. Instant bedroom. When we switch off the light, it is completely black inside.

"Maybe now," she says, feeding him his bottle, "he'll sleep."

He does. We don't. I lie awake and feel the earth make its huge revolutions beneath the bed.

What is Rome? Clouds. Church bells. The distant pin-pricks of birds. In Trastevere yesterday, a girl in a black dress sat on the rim of a fountain and scribbled into a leather book with a bright blue quill two feet long.

We meet some Academy fellows: a scholar of Latin epics named Maura, a lawyer-turned-composer named Harold, an abstract painter named Jackie. Many speak Italian, some are Latinists, too. Rebecca is studying a certain set of floor mosaics, Jessica a 1551 map. Jennifer is studying how Trojan myths were depicted in Roman paintings; Tony is studying the terra-cotta sculptures of Gianlorenzo Bernini. Rome, it seems, seeds esoteric passions: there are scholars of staircases, scholars of keyholes. A few years ago a fellow spent an entire year studying a handful of medieval coins; another spent two years examining the urban development of Parma between 1150 and 1350.

We meet the various gatekeepers, Luca, Lorenzo, a grizzled American expatriate named Norm. I carry Henry past the top-floor studios to the roof of the Academy, maybe fifty feet higher than the terrace of our apartment, the highest spot on the Janiculum, high enough to see over the iron cross at the very top of the Fontanone, high enough, it seems, to see the edge of the world. It is evening and the wind pours over us and the whole city looks spectral, insubstantial. As we watch, two clouds uncouple and a fan of sunlight surges through the gap, sending a wave of orange across the domes, crashing against the sides of apartment buildings, breaking across a mass of white marble that I think is the huge shrine to unified Italy called the Vittorio Emanuele II monument.

Everything is radiant. Distant trees toss; faraway walls gleam. The mountains at the horizon have switched on like streetlights, stark and defined, giving way to still more distant ranges.

Then everything goes dark again, the clouds knitted together, the mountains sucked back into silhouette, Rome sinking into shadow.

Mornings I try to get to work early, hurrying down the long, red-carpeted hallway on the second floor of the Academy, past dozens of closed doors. Behind them sleep visiting scholars and the fellows who don't have children, Franco the oil painter, John the architect. I unlock the Tom Andrews Studio, drag open the big window. Pliny's *Natural History,* the field guide to trees, and the war book sit on the desk; two pencils wait in the drawer. A few notes for my novel flutter on the cot.

I paper one wall with grainy photos of bombed-out cities. Saint-Lô. Dresden. Hamburg. I read about the Allied assault on Germany, incendiaries, firestorms, infernos so hungry for oxygen they sucked trees from the ground and human beings through walls. Beyond the windowsill, chimney swifts dip and turn over the garden. I open a notebook, sharpen a pencil. Paint flakes off the baseboards; a spider crouches in her web in a corner of the ceiling.

Some mornings, this is as far as I get.

We've been in Italy a week when a car kills two pedestrians a hundred yards from our front door. Our windows are open and I am putting a jar of baby food into the microwave when I hear the smack.

It is one of those noises you know instantly is a bad noise. There are sirens, more than usual. We carry the twins down to the sidewalk and watch the fire trucks, the ambulance, the insurance man taking photographs. A little rental Peugeot is smashed against the stone corner of the Porta San Pancrazio, the big archway at the end of our street.

The pedestrians were in a crosswalk. Parents of a ten-year-old, who was walking with them. The Peugeot was driven by an American tourist in his seventies. Both the tourist and his wife are hospitalized, in shock. As is the boy.

In our week here I have pushed Henry and Owen through that intersection three or four times a day. Yesterday, in a rainstorm, Shauna and I stopped the stroller beneath the Porta San Pancrazio and studied our map while traffic splashed past all around us.

Go to Rome, rent a compact, decimate a family. One instant, like any other, but in any particular instant everything can change. Obvious, perhaps, but it's one thing to think I understand this, and another to stand in our kitchen and hear it.

All afternoon I feel like lifting the boys out of the stroller and holding them against my chest. Sunlight filters through the olive trees in the garden, and the Street of the Four Winds down by the bakery comes alive with blowing leaves. In the evening I lift Owen high in the air and yell, "Crazy cannibal," and he squeals as I pretend to take bites out of his stomach.

Reinhold, a Venetian scholar studying centuries-old financial records in the studio next to mine, has a silver beard and an impossibly kind face and always wears corduroy. He tells me, in English, that parrots sometimes visit the garden. You have to be up early, he says. Keep your eyes out the window.

Parrots? The boys wake us before dawn every day; I have not yet missed a sunrise. Most days our little family is awake, I think, before every other person on the Janiculum Hill. The window in Reinhold's studio overlooks the same wedge of the back garden that my window does. But I haven't seen any parrots.

Flyers appear on Academy bulletin boards, a trip to ancient Ostia, a tour of something called the Cloaca Maxima. Am I supposed to know what these attractions are? The sign-up sheets are completely full of names anyway. Shauna and I bring the boys to an Academy lunch, six or seven tables arrayed in a corner of the courtyard. Around us are academics, scholars, a visiting luminary in rumpled linen.

". . . but the ecology of formal systems in Italian gardens prevents . . ."

". . . consider public religiosity . . ."

". . . of course Piranesi is about spectacle as much as . . ."

I hear someone—a classicist from California—at the table behind us say, very clearly, "You haven't been to Arch of Janus Quadrifrons yet?"

Henry bangs a spoon on the table; Owen dribbles milk down his chin. All the time here, it seems, we're missing things. I still have to stop myself from calling the Pantheon the Parthenon. We've been in Rome nearly two weeks and still haven't seen the Vatican.

Instead, we wrangle mashed bananas into the mouths of our sons. We wait ten minutes outside the office to ask the Academy's assistant director of operations, Pina, if she knows a shop in the city where we might buy crib bumpers.

At night Rome bangs, roars, peals. Car alarms, the shunting of a distant train, backfiring Fiats—at 2 a.m., someone below our window sets off a string of firecrackers. At three, the trash truck grinds up the street, upends the Dumpsters across from our front gate, and drops them again onto the asphalt.

Our building funnels noise strangely, too: a chair leg squeaking in the upstairs apartment, a door slamming downstairs, a girl's laughter clear as day through the wall behind our headboard. Even when the twins are sleeping quietly, I spring up in bed, thinking I've heard them wake up.

I shake Shauna's shoulder. "Are they crying? Which one is that?"

She groans. She stays asleep.

When the boys first came home from the hospital, six months ago, they had to be fed every three hours: three, six, nine, noon, three, six, nine, midnight. They were slow nursers and Shauna was breast-feeding eight hours a day. Owen had acid reflux and had to be given drops of Zantac every few hours. Henry had to be strapped to an apnea monitor the size of a VCR that squealed like a smoke detector any time his breathing paused or the adhesive on a diode slipped off his chest. The doctor had us put caffeine in his milk.

Once or twice a night, during those first weeks as a father, I would be drifting toward something like sleep when Henry's monitor would start screeching. The dog would leap trembling into the corner, Shauna would bolt upright, and I'd be scrambling out of bed, thinking, *He stopped breathing, he stopped breathing,* only to find Henry sound asleep and a loose diode stuck to the inside of his pajamas.

After a month it got so we could not remember whose diaper had been changed, who had been given what medicine, or even what day it was. There were nights when Owen screamed from dusk until dawn. There were nights when we had poured enough milk bottles and changed enough diapers and stayed awake enough consecutive hours that the rituals seemed to become somehow consecrated. I would stand dry-eyed over Henry as he stared up at the ceiling at three or four in the morning, and in something like a waking dream he would seem so wise and sensible that he became like some ancient philosopher.

He never cried, not even when his alarm went off. Swaddled in his Moses basket, wires trailing out the bottom, his monitor flashing green, green, green, his entire four-pound body motionless except his eyelids, it seemed he understood everything I was working so hard to understand: his mother's love, his brother's ceaseless crying; he was already forgiving me for my shortcomings as a father; he was the distillation of a dozen generations, my grandpa's grandpa's grandpa, all stripped into a single flame and stowed still-burning inside the thin slip of his ribs. I'd hold him at the window and he'd stare out into the night, blue tributaries of veins pulsing in his neck, his big eyelids slipping down now and then, and it would feel as if tethers were falling away, and the two of us were gently rising, through the glass, through the trees, through interweaving layers of atmosphere, into whatever was beyond the sky.

Occasionally I'd be lucid enough to think: This is not normal. I should not be trying to write a book during this.

By summer, after they were three or four months old, the boys started sleeping better at night. Four hours. Sometimes five. There were even one or two rare and terrifying times when both would sleep six hours without waking. But by then it was too late. So many nights of sleeplessness had broken some flimsy little gyroscope inside my skull, and the rested world had left me behind.

I'd lie awake and the clock beside the bed would flip through the minutes, click, breathe, click, breathe, and the moon would crawl across the panes of the windows. I'd worry the boys were suffocating in their blankets, I'd worry over the impending publication of my second book, I'd worry about September and moving to Rome. I'd worry I was worrying too much. I tried Unisom, exercise, alcohol. I tried thinking the same word over and over, *blue blue blue blue blue rain rain rain rain rain*. Shauna would take both boys all night, offering to, as we called it, throw herself under the bus, but still I'd lie awake, pillows clamped over my ears, heart roaring.

The only way to fall asleep is to stop trying to fall asleep. Sleep is a horizon: the harder you row toward it, the faster it recedes.

Now we have moved to Rome, my second book has just been published, and it is happening again. I stare at the ceiling, I paddle for the horizon, I hear what I am sure is a screaming baby. I tiptoe down the hall in the darkness and listen outside their doors. Nothing. Phantoms. Ghosts.

Our first storm: Lightning lashes the domes of churches. Hail clatters on the terrace. In the early morning, the air seems shinier and purer than I've seen it. Dawn stretches across the gardens, pulling tiny shadows out of the blades of grass, draining through the needles of the umbrella pines. The old walls look washed, almost new: a thousand speckled tints of bronze, trailing lacework of ivy, glossy tangles of capers.

We walk to the Vatican. It's closer than we expected, maybe five hundred yards along the rim of the Janiculum, past a huge statue of the nineteenth-century patriot Giuseppe Garibaldi on horseback, past dozens of stone busts of Garibaldi's lieutenants, past a children's hospital. We descend a steep alley, slip beneath an archway, skirt some shuttered restaurants. Suddenly St. Peter's and its vast piazza are upon us: the twin arms of a pillared colonnade, a ring of saints standing sentry around its circumference, a massive obelisk in the very center sending a needle-tipped shadow across a knot of tourists. The boys are quiet, huge-eyed. Twin fountains spray and gurgle. I feel my breath leave me, a flood of different sensations: the roar of space; sunlight coming in streaks through the haze; the huge dome of the church seeming almost to hover above the façade. It is as if, while we look, the basilica expands, swells, adds another layer. Country, continent: the piazza is a prairie, the church a mountain range. And the city crowds in all around it, panting, thronging, sulfurous.

That evening we eat tortellini on the terrace in a daze. Henry falls asleep in my arms. The sky passes through a sequence of darkening blues.

Is *this* Rome? Or a dream?

Streetlights blink on. A block away, the Fontanone roars over the city. As I'm setting Henry in his crib, a lone church bell, somewhere beyond his window, begins to clang.

We interview a babysitter. We have found her telephone number on wantedinrome.com. *Filipina, referenced and experienced babysitter, speaks English and Italian, looking for an afternoon job.* She knocks quietly and takes off her shoes before entering. Her name is Tacy. She has a son, back in the Philippines, who is fourteen. She has not seen him in two years. Her socks are navy blue. In under a minute we have run out of questions. She sits on the edge of the couch and holds her glass of water with two hands. What else are we supposed to ask?

"We need two or three afternoons a week," Shauna says. "And a night once in a while. We'd like to see some things around the city. We haven't even been to the Colosseum yet."

Tacy hasn't been to the Colosseum either. She has been working in Rome for two years, changing the diapers of an old man who has finally died. She likes to buy silver at the flea markets. She likes to read. Her leather jacket smells faintly of cigarettes. Before she came here, she had been a pharmaceutical rep in the Philippines, traveling between islands. Even then, she had to continually leave her son.

"Was it hard for you to come here?" I ask.

"Maybe fifty minutes by bus. Not far."

No, I want to clarify, was it hard for you to leave home, leave your son, but Shauna gives me a look. So I walk Tacy back down the hall, tiptoeing past the closed doors, the sleeping babies.

She slips on her shoes and points at Owen's door. "May I see?"

"It's a bathroom." I shrug. "It's darker in there."

We stand over the crib in the gloom. Owen is asleep facedown, sink on one side, tub on the other. His back rises and falls. His fan whirs.

"I hope I get this job," she whispers.

"I do, too," I say.

In the Tom Andrews Studio I try to research German occupations, revivify my characters, coax my imagination onto a hillside in Normandy, but my brain is tired, my eyes are sandy. Words unmoor from their locations on the page and drift, turn, slide toward the margin.

Supposedly, while performing the crucial calculations in his theory of general relativity, Einstein slept ten hours a night. I struggle to get five. Here's a headline from the newspaper: *Marriage and Children Kill Creativity in Men?* Two-thirds of "great" male scientists, reports some evolutionary psychologist in New Zealand, made their most significant contributions before their mid-thirties and before starting a family. Wonderful. Here's Einstein himself: "A person who has not made his great contribution to science before the age of thirty will never do so." What if all this is true, I wonder, for male writers?

I'm thirty-one. Here's Coleridge, in 1804, when he turned thirty-two: "Yesterday was my Birth Day. So completely has a whole year passed, with scarcely the fruits of a month.—O Sorrow and Shame. . . . I have done nothing!"

I haven't finished a piece of fiction since the boys were born. I want to write about the French radio resistance, but can't speak French, have never operated an old radio, and can't imagine how a Frenchman might talk in 1940, or even what he might carry in his pockets. When I look at copies of my first two books, even the novel published last month, they seem like strange and reticent objects; the paragraphs feel as though a lost brother has written them, a brother with much more time on his hands.

And now there's Rome, beginning to seep into everything, flooding my notebooks: the slumbering palaces, the hallucinatory light. *I never tire of the clouds here,* I've written across the top of a sheet of paper, *the light bleeding through their shoulders.*

Or this: *Through a window in Monteverde: a ladle smokes on a butcher's block.*

Yesterday I scribbled this: *Crossing the Ponte Sisto, over the Tiber, the air fills with shining threads. I wave my hands, squint. Is the light itself separating? For a minute I watch, the babies squirming in the stroller. Then I realize: They are spiderwebs, a tiny spider dangling from the end of each, all of them ballooning downriver.*

Every time I turn around here, I witness a miracle: wisteria pours up walls; slices of sky show through the high arches of a bell tower; water leaks nonstop from the spouts of a half-sunken marble boat in the Piazza di Spagna. A church floor looks soft as flesh; the skin from a ball of mozzarella cheese tastes rich enough to change my life. I ought to be reading about Vichy, collaborators and resisters, the albatross of military occupation. Instead I sit in the studio, open Pliny the Elder's *Natural History* for the first time, and read passages at random. "When the collapse of a building is imminent," he writes, "the mice migrate in advance, and spiders with their webs are the first things to fall." I flip forward a few hundred pages: "Athletes when sluggish are revitalized by love-making," he claims, "and the voice is restored from being gruff and husky. Sexual intercourse cures pain in the lower regions, impaired vision, unsoundness of mind and depression."

How can fiction compete with this guy? I carry a note-book to the roof of the Academy and try only to explain the complexion of stones, the distant blues of the Alban Hills, the lines of landscape.

The gaze widens and drifts; the eye is insatiable. The brain drowns.

We interview another babysitter, an Australian girl who says she is here in Rome "to party." Then we hire Tacy. She arrives the next afternoon and says she'll watch the babies for as many hours as we need. Shauna and I descend into the city clutching the address of a children's store. We walk miles, get lost twice. We ascend an artery called via Nazionale, an infinity of silk shirts and shoe shops, plunging staircases on our right, mannequin after mannequin modeling in windows. Energy pours off the traffic, off the sidewalks; it feels as if we are pumping through the interior of a living cell, mitochondria careering around, charged ions bouncing off membranes, everything arranging and rearranging.

Here is a pair of stone lions with crossed paws; here is a Gypsy sleeping on a square of cardboard. Down the white throat of a street a church floats atop stairs. A town car slows beside us, a gloved hand on the wheel, red lace in the backseat, a Siamese cat on the rear window ledge. Outside a hotel, a man with a bellows camera on a tripod ignites his flashbulb.

How old it all seems! And how new!—centuries bursting past in flashes, generations pouring along the streets like tides, old women, baby carriages, Caesars, popes, Mussolini—time is a bright scarf rippling past our eyes, columns rearing and toppling, temples rising and silting over and rising again.

We share a piece of pizza *con funghi* so full of flavor it forces our eyes closed: the oil in the crust tastes like sun and wind; then there is the salty cheese, and the deep-woods taste of oyster mushrooms.

It's dark when we find the children's store. Everything is very nice and very expensive. They have one backpack baby-carrier and one playpen in stock. We spend too much on both, carry them into the street, and climb into a taxi to go home.

Piazza Venezia rattles toward us on the left, the hub of Rome, no traffic lights, buses swarming round pedestrians, a policeman on a box orchestrating everything with white gloves. The soaring marble ledges of the Victor Emmanuel II Monument—the Vittoriano, Altar of the Fatherland, a colossal cascade of marble platforms—loom above us, ten thousand tons of *botticino* limestone. Fifty or sixty gulls ride the wind above the chariots on its roof, three hundred feet above the street. They turn slow circles in the spotlights, never lowering their wings. Ghosts, or angels.

Not until we're back in our apartment building, riding the elevator, do we realize we only know Tacy's first name and her cell phone number.

The stairwell is dark. The apartment door is locked. My heart disintegrates in my chest. We will never see our sons again. I will have to talk to uninterested police captains; I will have to learn the Italian word for *abduction*. I will carry Henry's pacifier in my pocket for the rest of my anemic, broken life. I will have to tell my mother, "Well, we found her on the Internet . . ."

Shauna slides her key into the lock. We creep down the hall. The boys are sitting on a blanket on the floor with their toys. They smile at us. Tacy smiles. Everything—the little round table, the counters, the bottles in the sink—has been cleaned.

October wanes. We have lived in Italy almost a month. At the Palazzo Senatorio, a twelfth-century palace in the Campidoglio, right next to the Vittoriano, six hundred dignitaries stand in their dark suits and listen to each other endorse the constitution of the European Union. Five thousand security people; two tractor trailers stuffed with flowers. In the afternoon two stretched-out BMWs race past us on the street, each escorted by three police sedans, sirens turning, black windows flashing past.

Pomp, power, importance. I sit in the Tom Andrews Studio and read chapter after chapter of Pliny's *Natural History*. He is half-genius, half-lunatic. It is as though

Borges has rewritten Aristotle, patched in some Thoreau, then airmailed it to Calvino to revise.

Pliny the Elder was born in AD 23; he became a cavalry officer, then commander of an entire army. He was chubby, fond of baths, hardly slept. By age thirty-six, he'd completed three works: a treatise on how to throw spears from horseback, a biography of a friend, and a history of the Germanic wars in twenty volumes. But the *Natural History* was his magnum opus and is his only extant work. Completed in AD 77, it consists of thirty-seven separate books and addresses everything from geography to crystallography to the ability of hyenas to spontaneously change their gender. His subject is the universe, from stars all the way down to polyps, and ultimately what the *Natural History* presents is a panorama of an ancient world crawling with myth and misinformation, but also elegant and ordered and deeply beautiful.

The more pages I turn, the more I find an endearing sweetness in Pliny; he is so curious, so ardent. The elephant's "natural gentleness toward those not so strong as itself," he writes, "is so great that if it gets among a flock of sheep it will remove with its trunk those that come in its way, so as not unwittingly to crush one."

Later he marvels, "Where did Nature find a place in a flea for all the senses?"

I descend into the Academy library, find the complete *Natural History* translated and unabridged, and borrow as many volumes as I can carry.

For Halloween we dress the boys as a lion and a dog and stroll them to the Piazza Navona, an elongated oval in the center of the city packed with cafés and fountains. The streets swirl with light. Shadows flicker and waver like candle flames; the sides of houses, caught by the sun, glow like embers. Crows (all black like American crows, except Italian ones have gray on their backs, as if they wear a sweater tied around their necks) hop through the piazza and pick through blowing trash. All through the historic center, even though it's eighty degrees, Romans model leather coats. We sit on a stair outside an apartment; Shauna unzips her backpack and mixes our last two bottles of American baby formula. Shutters bang and the engine noise of the city rinses everything else away.

All week I try to force myself to set aside Pliny and fiddle with scraps of my novel. I spend a half hour changing a character's name across four pages of text, then finish out the hour by changing it back to the original name. Each morning the ice that has formed over my draft feels thicker, my initial enthusiasm fainter. Reality subsumes fiction; how can I write about France in the 1940s when the countless faces of Rome (in our 2004, in Pliny's 77) swarm all around me? The brittle crust of the present fractures; my feet sink into the quicksand of antiquity.

By noon I'm reading Pliny again. He is self-deprecating; he is scrutinizing things no previous Roman writer had ever paid much attention to: centipedes, pinecones, ravens. In his world comets, eclipses, thunderclaps, birds, fish, spiders, fig trees, natural springs, sneezes, and stumbles portend events; honey comes from air, butterflies are born from dew, cranes regularly assemble to hold symposiums, and moles tunneling beneath houses can understand what is being said above them. Lightning bolts make catfish drowsy, horses will burst open if they are ridden across wolf tracks, and dolphins "answer to the name of 'Snubnose' and like it better than any other."

But Pliny can be sweetly, perfectly astute, too. "Whales," he writes, "have their mouths in their foreheads and consequently when swimming on the surface of the water they blow clouds of spray into the air." He understands the earth is spherical; he carefully traces how daylight varies with latitude. And, fifteen hundred years before the invention of the microscope, he manages to make some sublime observations about insects, bees in particular.

Read a certain way, the *Natural History* is preposterous, full of erroneous assumptions and cast-off mythology. Read another way, it is a window into Roman understanding two millennia ago. Read another way, it is a tribute to wonder itself.

For the past sixteen years, pretty much every single day, I've penciled a journal entry into a spiral notebook. It is a practice field, an exercise bike; I write in it to try to stay in writing shape. In Boise, most mornings, I sit over a blank page and squeeze out a paragraph, then start writing fiction. During this first month in Italy, I sit down and two hours disappear and I've filled five pages.

I write in my notebooks, change diapers, buy groceries. I fry pancetta with a child strapped to my back. I conduct a phone interview with the *Washington Post* with a child strapped to my chest. By the time we bathe the boys, fight them into pajamas, and pile them into their cribs, it is usually seven thirty or eight. We cook dinner. We read. We go to bed. Twenty minutes later Shauna is asleep. I am not. I read about drool rash online, I try to decipher ingredients in Italian baby formula. *Idrolisato di caseina. Minerali enzimatici.* Are these good things to put into an infant?

I wander on and off the terrace, I try drawing pictures of trees in a notepad. On the National Sleep Foundation website I read, "In the long term, the clinical consequences of sleep deprivation are associated with numerous, serious medical illnesses, including . . . high blood pressure, heart attack, heart failure, stroke, psychiatric problems, mental impairment, and poor quality of life."

A bundle of marguerites, tied with black ribbon and leaning against the corner of the Porta San Pancrazio, has wilted and fallen to the pavement. I pick up the bouquet and reposition it against the stone, but it falls again, and I worry the drivers in the cars whizzing past will think I'm being disrespectful so I take the brake off the stroller and hurry home with the milk.

Saint Pancratius: fourteen years old when he was martyred. His job in heaven is to avenge perjurers.

It's the second of November, election day in the United States. Around noon a sudden wind slams my studio door and I hear the little framed sign (*The Tom Andrews Studio, Fellow, American Academy in Rome '00*) shatter on the tile in the hall. I open the door and pile slivers of glass into the trash can thinking, Omen. Pliny whispers in my ear, "Different days pass verdict on different men and only the last day a final verdict on all men; and consequently no day is to be trusted."

An hour later my editor e-mails to tell me the *New*

York Times will run a halfhearted review of my newly published novel on Sunday that includes the sentence "Doerr's interest in nature is so obsessive that the whole equation of man in nature becomes heavily skewed in favor of the latter, producing fiction of rapturous beauty but of an oddly cold, uninvolving nature, as if it were embalmed in its own lustrous style."

Great. *Embalm: to preserve a corpse from decay, originally with spices, now usually by the arterial injection of a preservative.* I blunder up the stairwell and into the apartment and stand over the toilet awhile, waiting for something to pass.

Still, after the boys are asleep, after dinner, I actually manage to fall into something like sleep. I dream of knights and haberdashers and a psychologist tapping a white pen on a red notebook. Around 5 a.m. Shauna wakes me to tell me George W. Bush has won Ohio and Florida and will be president of the United States for four more years.

Ten minutes later the boys are crying. We carry them in laps around the apartment and feed them milk. Henry grabs for my index finger and won't let go. A rash circling Owen's throat has descended his sternum and is now crowding his chest, pink and raw.

"Omens," I tell Shauna. "Don't you feel like everything is going to end badly?"

Henry settles down. The nipple of Owen's bottle collapses and formula dribbles onto his pajamas. He begins to cry again.

"Not everything," Shauna says.

The leaves of plane trees skid through the streets like pages from some strange and ancient manuscript. In a *latteria* near the Pantheon we buy a kilogram of Parmigiano for fourteen euros. The gray-haired proprietor, wearing his white coat, a scientist of cheese, hacks our wedge off a wheel the size of a spare tire. Sixteen liters of milk, he tells us, went into this one kilogram. He wraps it in cellophane and waxed paper. It sits in our refrigerator and glows, shot through with crystals like some fabled hunk of mineral. It tastes like nutmeg and brine and cream; we eat slices as if it were cake.

The botanist Carl Linnaeus, I read once, could tell the time of day by observing when certain flowers opened and closed in his garden. I gaze out my studio window, past the trunk of the umbrella pine. How does one get to be that involved in the world?

Reinhold is messing with me about the parrots, I'm sure of it.

In the middle of November I finally get our names onto one of the overloaded Academy sign-up sheets. We leave the boys with Tacy. From a courtyard in Campo Marzio, a neighborhood near the Pantheon, a composer named Lee Hyla leads a dozen Academy fellows into a dripping, cramped basement that smells of mold. Three of us at a time take turns peering from archaeologists' scaffolding at a patch of wet earth fifteen feet below. In a space the size of a small bedroom, beneath a film of water, is a sliver of a two-thousand-year-old sundial—markings on a piazza that was once a hundred meters across.

It is the Orologio of Augustus, Lee tells us. The sundial was oriented so that the shadow of an obelisk, long since moved to another part of the city, Piazza di Montecitorio, fell across the hour, day, and month. The hash marks were bronze rods inlaid in the paving, and the obelisk, like just about all the obelisks of Rome, had been stolen from Africa and brought across the Mediterranean on a barge.

Think of that sundial, all that bronze burning in the sun. Think of those barges, a 170-ton granite needle laid from bow to stern, wallowing in the sea.

This, I'm learning, is what the American Academy seems to be about: a bird-watching, expressionistic jazz composer from Boston teaching us about the solar clocks of emperors. I lie awake reading about obelisks, the obelisk of Ramses, the obelisk of Psammetichus II. History lies beneath the city like an extensive and complicated armature. Emperors were stabbed beneath tramlines. Sheep grazed beneath supermarkets. The thirteen obelisks of Rome have been toppled and reerected and shuffled around so many times that to lay a map of their previous positions over a map of their current ones is to evoke a miniature cross-hatching of the city's entire memory, a history of power and vanity like a labyrinth stamped beneath the streets.

I wander the library and read about Gianlorenzo Bernini, the seventeenth-century sculptor, painter, and architect who at ten years old was summoned in front of Paul V to draw a portrait (the pope asked Bernini to draw St. Paul and, upon seeing the result, declared the boy would "be the Michelangelo of his age"); who was already being commissioned to carve marble busts at age twelve; who carved the leaking stone boat in the Piazza di Spagna; who was the most celebrated artist of his age. Who could peer into the white cliffs of a marble quarry and see, trapped inside a block of stone, Neptune's forearm, say, or a coil of Persephone's hair.

I learn I prefer Bernini's recalcitrant rival, an ex-pupil named Francesco Borromini, a stonecutter's son, introverted, suicidal, insanely gifted. Bernini is polished, urbane, in love with the human body; Borromini is touchy, outlandish, more interested in pure geometry. Borromini's Saint Charles at the Four Fountains is a pocket-sized church at an exhaust-blackened intersection a mile or so from our apartment: its interior is stripped of ornament; hexagons, octagons, and crosses are planted in the dome; light strips away weight. You walk in, you feel as if you might float out of your shoes.

In Piazza Navona, Bernini's quartet of wet, muscled river gods, their fingers thicker than my wrists, balance on the rim of their fountain fifty feet east of Borromini's Church of St. Agnes: it is a 350-year-old architectural showdown. Bernini was theatrical, savvy, and connected; he had eleven children and a self-admitted "inclination to pleasure." He died rich. Borromini was difficult, confrontational, and constantly out of favor with the papacy. When he committed suicide in 1667, he was almost totally broke.

But in Rome, I'm learning, practically everything is set in opposition to something else—not only its most famous baroque architects, but its founding twins, the crypts beneath its churches, the hovels next to its palazzi, the empires within empires. Alleys rear and twist and cough up their cobblestones like big, black molars. A street one block is called via Carini and the next via Barrilli. F. Torre becomes A. Colautti. Halfway up a hill, Perotti transforms into Marino. We walk the street of light, the street of flowers, the street of crossbow makers. I look up and realize I have been here before. Still, I'm lost. Three nuns in a Jetta wait for us to pass and study the double stroller with gentle eyes.

"I think we go left here," I say, unfolding the map, and Shauna, shaking her head, leads us right, toward home.

We have days like this: On the way home from the supermarket, towing forty pounds of groceries in a handcart, I step dead center into a big piece of dog shit. Thirty minutes later Shauna drops a jar of mustard, which explodes on the kitchen floor and sends hundreds of mustardy glass fragments shooting across the tiles. Henry needs to be changed, Owen has woken up an hour too soon, a sinkful of bottles need to be washed, four dozen toys need to be put back in their cardboard box.

After dark I sit on the edge of the tub in Owen's bathroom-turned-bedroom and feed him his nighttime bottle. He sighs; his eyes get sleepy. I rest my toe on the base of his crib, and suddenly the entire side rail splits apart, slats falling everywhere. A half hour with Super Glue while Shauna bounces both infants, and finally the crib holds together and we lower in our son, and all night I lie awake and wait for the sounds of splintering.

Then we have days like this: I'm pushing the stroller when I see one yellow rose, plump and spotless, blooming thirty feet above the street on top of the Aurelian wall. The moon rides above Borromini's perfect clock tower on the via dei Filippini; in St. Peter's Square (really an ellipse), I sit between the trunks of pillars in Bernini's colonnade and write in my notebook beneath stripes of purple sky.

We cook hamburgers made from veal. We make a disastrously good tomato soup and shave half a pound of Parmigiano into it. We drink $4 bottles of Chianti. We buy lemon-flavored yogurt in little bell-shaped jars sold at a dairy down the street and feed our boys shining white spoonfuls.

I put my name onto another sign-up sheet. This time Shauna stays home while I get to creep with some other Academy fellows up the spiral staircase inside Trajan's column, a privilege that requires a *permesso,* months of carefully phrased correspondence, and a giant brass key. The column stands near the Vittoriano and is made from twenty marble drums, each around forty tons, stacked on top of each other one hundred feet high, carved on the outside with a 650-foot-long spiraling frieze detailing Emperor Trajan's various exploits: Trajan addressing troops, foes fleeing villages, fortifications being happily constructed. It is his ratified history, his political billboard, his public memoir. Earthquakes, windstorms, a half dozen military occupations—in 1,893 years, nothing has toppled it.

Another monument to ego that has become, over time, a monument to craftsmanship and wonder itself, such as the obelisks, Augustus's sundial, or the triumphal arches marking the Forum. For me it does not conjure an image of Trajan nearly as much as it conjures an image of the promenade of all that Carrara marble: eight hundred tons of it, sailed down half the coast of Italy, barged up the Tiber, carted through the heaving, crowded streets, the straining horses, the creaking ropes.

A little door at the column's base opens; five or six of us duck to enter. We climb one by one toward a tiny railing at the top. One hundred and eighty-five steps. It smells like cold limestone and mildew. The tiny windows, one every quarter turn, show only sky. There is graffiti in there four times older than the United States. And to the visitors who put it there, Trajan's column was already ancient. I creep out the trapdoor on top and stand at the brink of a cliff: the column invisible below, the ruins of the various forums spread in front. Everything is solemn and sparkling: the lost temples and shells of markets, the hard-won stones of Empire imperceptibly resolving themselves back into the earth.

"Headlands are laid open to the sea," Pliny wrote, "and nature is flattened. We remove the barriers created to serve as the boundaries of nations, and ships are built specially for marble. And so, over the waves of the sea, Nature's wildest element, mountain ranges are transported to and fro."

I think: Idaho will never look the same. I think: Maybe what glitters in the air above this city are souls, so many of them rising from this same earth that they become visible, get shuffled around in the wind, get blown thirty miles west, and settle across the shining plains of the Tyrrhenian Sea.

Thanksgiving: our first as parents. Giant silver clouds fly above the terrace. Sudden shocks of light avalanche through the windows. Seconds later the shadows return. Rome: a contest between sun and shadow, kingdom and time, architecture and weeds. The shadows will win, of course, and time, and weeds. But this morning the match seems close.

I let Shauna sleep in, zip the boys into their thick blue fleeces, and carry them down the stairwell. I push their stroller past the Porta San Pancrazio, down Carini, down the Street of the Four Winds. It is odd to see shops opening and commuters racing to work; it is my first Thanksgiving, I realize, outside of the United States.

At the bakery there is a small triumph: no queue. Men slide big stainless trays in and out of racks. I ask for four croissants and four pieces of pizza *rossa,* small, cheeseless squares of crust, paper-thin, brushed with tomatoes. A baker crouches and waggles a flour-white finger at the boys: *"Buongiorno!"* Before we leave, three of his coworkers have joined him, sitting on their heels and admiring the babies to one another.

We head not back home but for the bus stop. Cats slink behind Dumpsters. A man on a balcony waters geraniums. Through an open window, one floor up, I see a woman in her kitchen scrubbing carrots with a yellow brush.

A half dozen Romans stop me: "They are twins?" "How many years do they have?" "Where did you buy that stroller?" Half my Italian vocabulary has to do with baby gear.

Near the vegetable market we pass a man holding hands with a little girl. She gazes at the boys with a bright, impersonal wonder. Her father whispers something to her as they pull even with us; she laughs; it is as if skeins of love are passing invisibly between them. And suddenly the gulf between me and the Italians of the neighborhood seems navigable—I want to follow the man and his daughter and ask them things. Which of these buildings do you live in? What could I cook with this zucchini I've bought? Have you seen the Orologio of Augustus?

But I don't, and soon they are a block away. All I can manage are smiles and sentence fragments anyway. I try a *"Buongiorno"* on the guard outside a bank and he scowls back, fierce and ridiculous all at once, his big handgun looming on his hip. Beneath the window of a wine shop, two stores farther along, someone has spray-painted, in English, *BUSH GO HOME.*

Barricades reemerge: language, culture, time. To be a nonfluent foreigner is to pass through one gate only to find yourself outside two more.

I wrestle the stroller onto the #75 bus. It rattles down switchbacks into Trastevere; it groans across the Tiber. Owen coos and moans. Henry sucks his pacifier. After maybe three more stops, I wheel them off in a neighborhood called Testaccio, near the metro station. I ring a bell outside what I hope is the Protestant cemetery, one of the oldest continually used burial grounds in Europe. An old man swings open the gate.

Inside are umbrella pines, box hedges, headstones in clusters. The pyramid of Cestius, a magistrate's tomb from the first century BC, looms half inside the walls, its marble-faced blocks mottled with weather and lichen. Crumpled leaves blow across the paths, and big, dusky cypress trees creak like masts.

John Keats, whose grave I want to see, is buried near the corner. The stone reads:

This Grave contains all that was mortal, of a Young English Poet, who on his Death Bed, in the Bitterness of his heart, at the Malicious Power of his enemies, desired these words to be Engraven on his Tomb Stone: Here lies One Whose Name was writ in Water.

Keats died in a little room beside the Spanish Steps, two miles north of here, within earshot of Bernini's perpetually leaking marble boat. It was 1821; he was twenty-six; tuberculosis had stalked his family for years.

Here lies One Whose Name was writ in Water. Did he mean that to write your name in stone is vanity? That all of us, foreigners or locals, are ultimately anonymous?

The tombs sleep heavily in the grass. The babies squirm. I gaze down rows of memorials into silent corners. We are hemmed by brickwork, ivy, history. A line from a Tom Andrews poem comes back to me: "The dead drag a grappling hook for the living. The hook is enormous."

As far as I can tell, Henry, Owen, and I are the only people here. It's serene, but disquieting, too; it feels as though we are vastly outnumbered. Again I feel, acutely, that we are outsiders—that there are things in Rome that I will never come close to understanding. The grappling hook drags through the trees, the lawn. I want, suddenly, to get my sons away from here.

On the bus home I hold Owen at the window, put my finger in Henry's fist. Owen leans his head against my neck and sighs. I get off in Monteverde, wheel them home. In the elevator they smile into the mirror from beneath their hoods. We rise through the stairwell. Owen reaches for the bakery bag in my fist. Henry fumbles for the keys.

I heap the boys onto their mother. They laugh and laugh. We eat our croissants; we drink pineapple juice from a box. Yesterday, Shauna tells me, Owen clapped his hands twice. Henry can now roll halfway across the room.

That evening I am reading Pliny in my studio when two parrots, bottle green, flash across the lawn below the window. They are there so suddenly I am disoriented: Is this Italy? Or the Amazon? Their size confuses scale; they are like fat, green herons; their wingspan looks as if it is as wide across as my desk.

They circle the garden once, one above and slightly in front of the other, screeching to one another. Then they dip over the wall and are swallowed by the trees.

What do I give thanks for this Thanksgiving? The boys, and Shauna, and the veal meatballs the butcher rolls in bread crumbs and packs in waxed paper. I'm thankful for music and the taste of the little chocolate coffee cups from the *cioccolateria* Shauna found in Trastevere, and the heat from the radiator beside me, and for the pencil box Shauna bought me two days ago made out of handmade paper. I'm thankful that everything sweet is sweet because it is finite.

WINTER

THE EARTH TRUNDLES ALONG. AUTUMN SEEPS away from Rome. Good-bye, tomatoes; good-bye, tourists. Good-bye, whitethroats and warblers, and good-bye to the little brown corn bunting who landed on our terrace yesterday and sang a few notes before continuing on. Tonight I press my face into the pillow and imagine the migrants sweeping south through Europe, down the length of Italy, swallows and kingfishers, bean geese and sand martins, a tide across the Alps, darkening the moon, chasing the sun.

The vegetable stand we buy from is located in a little convergence of alleys between the hardware store and the bakery, called Largo Luigi Micelli. The sisters who run it are stubby-fingered and wear gumboots. *"Buongiorno,"* they say, every time we arrive. *"Dimmi."* Tell me.

Most days a son helps them, eager and grave in his apron, periodically bringing a hand to his upper lip to confirm the existence of his downy mustache. The three of them educate me in winter produce: one type of cauliflower white as cotton, another purple as dusk; sheaves of young leeks with mud still packed in their roots; basins of squash; tiny, spherical potatoes like miniature moons. Frost, they say, adds flavor to the leaves of kale; winter radicchio should be brushed with oil and grilled on warm coals. There is fennel in bright, reedy piles. Crinkly, soft cabbages. Mountains of radishes. There are eggplants in rows and eggplants in heaps; indigo, violet-blue, some so purple they are black.

The leeks are bundled like debarked, nascent trees; the red-leaf lettuces are aloof and silent; they burn like torch flames. Especially in wet weather the market is luminous: the air slightly smoky, the stalls seemingly huddled together against the chill, the emerald piles of spinach, the orange pyramids of carrots, a dozen tattered umbrellas gleaming with beads of rain. And then, at noon, shutters are drawn, awnings collapse, the banquet is put away, and in the evening we walk past on the way home from a restaurant and all that remains of the market are locked stalls and trash in the gutters and the reflections of streetlights in the puddles.

This morning the sisters have wood strawberries, *fragoline di bosco,* little red droplets of flesh. They have supposedly been harvested in the hills we can see from the roof of the Academy.

I buy a carton for two euros, then reach inside the stroller's rain cover and hand a strawberry like a tiny glowing lamp to each of the boys. They study it before sliding it between their lips.

In 1976, a doctoral student at the University of Nottingham in England demonstrated that randomizing letters in the middle of words had no effect on the ability of readers to understand sentences. In tihs setncene, for emalxpe, ervey scarbelmd wrod rmenias bcilasaly leibgle. Why? Because we are deeply accustomed to seeing letters arranged in certain patterns. Because the eye is in a rush, and the brain, eager to locate meaning, makes assumptions.

This is true of phrases, too. An author writes "crack of dawn" or "sidelong glance" or "crystal clear" and the reader's eye continues on, at ease with combinations of words it has encountered innumerable times before. But does the reader, or the writer, actually expend the energy to see what is cracking at dawn or what is clear about a crystal?

The mind craves ease; it encourages the senses to recognize symbols, to gloss. It makes maps of our kitchen drawers and neighborhood streets; it fashions a sort of algebra out of life. And this is useful, even essential—X is the route to work, Y is the heft and feel of a nickel between your fingers. Without habit, the beauty of the world would overwhelm us. We'd pass out every time we saw— actually *saw*—a flower. Imagine if we only got to see a cumulonimbus cloud or Cassiopeia or a snowfall once a century: there'd be pandemonium in the streets. People would lie by the thousands in the fields on their backs.

We need habit to get through a day, to get to work, to feed our children. But habit is dangerous, too. The act of seeing can quickly become unconscious and automatic. The eye sees something—gray-brown bark, say, fissured into broad, vertical plates—and the brain spits out *tree trunk* and the eye moves on. But did I really take the time to see the tree? I glimpse hazel hair, high cheekbones, a field of freckles, and I think *Shauna*. But did I take the time to see my wife?

"Habitualization," a Russian army-commissar-turned-literary-critic named Viktor Shklovsky wrote in 1917, "devours works, clothes, furniture, one's wife, and the fear of war." What he argued is that, over time, we stop perceiving familiar things—words, friends, apartments—as they truly are. To eat a banana for the thousandth time is nothing like eating a banana for the first time. To have sex with somebody for the thousandth time is nothing like having sex with that person for the first time. The easier an experience, or the more entrenched, or the more familiar, the fainter our sensation of it becomes. This is true of chocolate and marriages and hometowns and narrative structures. Complexities wane, miracles become unremarkable, and if we're not careful, pretty soon we're gazing out at our lives as if through a burlap sack.

In the Tom Andrews Studio I open my journal and stare out at the trunk of the umbrella pine and do my best to fight off the atrophy that comes from seeing things too frequently. I try to shape a few sentences around this tiny corner of Rome; I try to force my eye to slow down. A good journal entry—like a good song, or sketch, or photograph—ought to break up the habitual and lift away the film that forms over the eye, the finger, the tongue, the heart. A good journal entry ought be a love letter to the world.

Leave home, leave the country, leave the familiar. Only then can routine experience—buying bread, eating vegetables, even saying hello—become new all over again.

In early December we are talking to Laura in the basement laundry room when she tells us this: if it ever begins to snow, we should run to the Pantheon, because to see snowflakes come drifting through the hole at the top of the dome is to change your life forever.

Shauna holds Henry on her hip and—with one hand—folds another basket of laundry. She asks, "Haven't our lives already been changed forever?"

Still, in the mornings I find myself creeping onto the terrace to inspect the sky. Is today the day? Is tomorrow? Maybe, I think, although there is no logic to it, if I see snow come through the roof of the Pantheon, I'll finally be able to sleep.

"It hasn't snowed in Rome in four years," Lorenzo, the gatekeeper, tells me. He sits in the *portineria,* the gatekeeper's lodge, in a parka. A space heater blows onto his shoes. *"Grazie a Dio,"* he adds. Thank God.

"Does the city even have snowplows?" I ask.

He cocks his head. Behind his glasses his eyeballs are intensely magnified, twice the size they should be. "What do you mean, *snowplows*?"

Halfway to the studio, I stop in the courtyard. The square of sky above me is a roiling silver, and there is frost in the jasmine, and the water in the fountain looks slow and thick, like cooling wax. As if any moment structures of ice might start lacing their way across the top. As if any moment the sky might send down a few wandering crystals.

December 8 is the Feast of the Immaculate Conception. All morning the air is filled with bells, and a parade of nuns marches up via Carini in the rain. Crows drift over the terrace, silent and threadbare, like deposed kings. Out in the street Laura's husband, Jon, the landscape architect, drags a tree stump toward his studio. Celia, a classicist, stands outside the Academy's front gate, wiping rain from her eyeglasses.

Across town, next to the McDonald's in Piazza di Spagna, children offer roses to a bronze Madonna on a pillar. The pope is wheeled out of his car to pray at her feet.

The rain picks up. By afternoon, nightcrawlers, thick as fingers, have washed onto the sidewalks. They are huge, the kind of worms you usually see only in bait shops, and it is a little unnerving. Looking at them, I wonder what other hidden things are issuing out of the lawns.

We heave the stroller on and off a bus. Near Oviesse, a department store in Trastevere, a massive dog, a Newfoundland, maybe a hundred pounds, barks as his owner locks a leash into the compartment over the rear bumper of a *motorino*. Bark, bark, says the dog. The man says something back.

The dog circles the scooter, sniffing. The man lights a cigarette and puts on a helmet and finally seats himself and nods to the dog—hardly a motion with his chin—and the dog scrambles onto the tiny platform in front of the man's feet. Strings of drool swing from his jaw.

The man starts the *motorino*. Cigarette still in his teeth, without checking his mirrors, man and dog race into the traffic on viale Trastevere. Beads of water shine on the cobbles, and on the umbrellas of pedestrians, and on the windshield of a tram as it groans to a stop beside us.

The oldest building in Idaho with its original roof still intact is the Mission of the Sacred Heart, just off I-90 near

Cataldo, three hundred miles north of Boise, built by Jesuits and Coeur d'Alene tribespeople in 1853. When you see it for the first time, you think: Gosh, that's pretty old. Forty feet high, no nails, handprints of native children still visible in the adobe. Timber had to be hauled in from a mile away. Foundation stones had to be chopped out of nearby mountains. Mud had to be dragged up from the river. You think: Life was pretty hard for those guys.

The oldest building in Rome with its original roof still intact is the Pantheon, rebuilt atop an older, fire-damaged temple by the emperor Hadrian around AD 125. When you see the Pantheon for the first time, your mind caves in.

Its doors are twenty-one feet high and weigh eight tons each. The sixteen columns on its porch are thirty-nine feet high and weigh about sixty tons each, roughly the weight of two fully loaded eighteen-wheelers, crushed and compacted into a cylinder five feet across. The columns were not hauled here from a mile away. They were quarried in eastern Egypt, dragged on sledges to the Nile, rowed across the Mediterranean, barged up the Tiber, and carted through the streets of Rome. They are ocean gray, flecked with mica, glassy and cold; it is impossible to be close to one and not want to touch it.

The vault of the Pantheon is made of concrete and has a diameter of 143 feet. The hole in the top, the oculus, is twenty-seven feet across. For thirteen centuries, it was the largest dome in the world. For nineteen centuries, it has resisted lightning strikes and earthquakes and barbarians.

But numbers, dimensions, facts—they come later. When you first see it, the Pantheon is about wonder. You walk through the gigantic doorway and your attention is sucked upward to a circle of sky. A filtering haze floats inside; a column of light strikes through the oculus and leans against the floor. The space is both intimate and explosive: your humanity is not diminished in the least, and yet simultaneously the Pantheon forces you to pay attention to the fact that the world includes things far greater than yourself.

The circular turret crowning the dome of St. Peter's is supposed to represent the all-seeing, all-knowing eye of God, but you can't help but feel, in the Pantheon, that the real eye is positioned directly over your head. You dwindle, you shrink; you teeter on the threshold of a vast, blue country.

Nineteen hundred years: invading armies, executions, and sacraments, the temple's foundations sliding in the marshy ground, countless houses rising and falling all around, the Tiber flooding it three or four times a year for centuries—and yet, here it stands.

I am the sheet of film in a pinhole camera; I am the fetus in the womb. Particles of dust swim in the sunlight. Something in my chest unwinds, something blooms.

Three and a half million people visit the Pantheon every year. I go there maybe six times in December, hoping to fit my mind around it, hoping for snow.

I pencil Italian vocabulary onto sheets of paper, seal them inside our last Ziploc bag, and tape them inside the shower. *Ho perso il biglietto.* I've lost my ticket. *Mi sono perso.* I've lost my way. To no avail: my Italian remains miserable. I back the big stroller through the door of the little grocery store, Beti, park it beside the shelves of cookies, fight to the front of the throng, and ask the grocer across the counter for tomato sauce.

"*Sugo di pompelmo,*" I say. "*Con basilico.*" She squints at me. She knows me, I think; several times she has offered Henry and Owen lollipops.

"*Sugo di pompelmo,*" I say. I point.

Her fingers float past the jars on the shelves.

"*Sugo di carne?*"

There are two dozen jars of tomato sauce right in front of her eyes. I speak more loudly. "*No, no. Sugo di pompelmo.*"

I am determined not to fail. She holds up a can of pears. I shake her off. She holds up jar of tomatoes with mushrooms. "*Questo? Pomodori? Con funghi?*"

"*Ecco!*" I say. "*Sì.*" With mushrooms. Good enough. She hands me the jar. I pay. It's not until I'm back on via Carini, halfway home, that I realize I was hollering for grapefruit sauce. Grapefruit sauce with basil.

On the Ponte Sisto, a fifteenth-century bridge built by Pope Sixtus IV, a dozen Africans carefully arrange their knockoff Prada purses on blankets, shining them, straightening them. Then they lean back on the balustrade on their elbows and talk. The lantern of St. Peter's glows orange in the distance.

We pass two disheveled guys with five dogs between them. The men bend over a camp stove upon which a pot steams: slaw, mounds of it, and a meter-long sausage, coiled over itself, boiled pink. An upside-down baseball cap sits in front of them, a few coins inside.

Pretty much all the panhandlers we've seen in Rome

have dogs: terriers, Great Danes, a black lab nursing a litter of piebald puppies. The strategy appears to be this: Put some sedated dogs on a blanket and use the first-person plural on your sign. *Please help us. We need food.*

Every time she sees the dogs, Shauna cries. Today a yellow Lab on a sheet of cardboard raises his head, watching us with flat eyes. The wind sticks a scrap of leaf against the side of his face, then wrenches it away. He is looking not so much at us as through us. One of his hind legs is missing.

Already I can sense Shauna tensing up, her lower lip quivering. I put my arm around her, push the stroller a bit faster, point at something at the far end of the bridge.

We construct schedules for Henry and Owen like bungling one-star generals. A nap at nine and another at two. Mid-morning snack. Midafternoon snack. Bath before bed. Every day one boy or the other is skipping his nap or falling asleep in the stroller long before he is supposed to. Neither seems very interested in food. Both want to be held all the time. Is this what it means to be a parent—to constantly fail to be in control of anything?

Late afternoons, as it's getting dark, after I've written a journal entry and read Pliny and added not one single worthwhile paragraph to my novel, I'll return home from the studio and take whichever boy happens to be awake out in the backpack to see the starlings.

Tonight I take Owen. We head downhill from the apartment, kicking up leaves, the frame of the carrier creaking in the cold. He hums a sustained C-sharp into my ear. We pause beside the piers of the Fontanone where the water is splashing blue and cold across the marble and cross via Garibaldi to look out at the city. A few tourists brave the cold. Traffic throbs past. The view still dazzles me, every time. Rome is orange. The sky is deep-ocean blue. Above the Albans, Venus shines a pale white.

Not quite black, not quite gray, in the hand a starling shimmers with greens and purples, like a puddle touched with oil. Lovely, but common, too, and the rampancy of starlings more than anything casts them as grimy, despised birds. They take over winter feeders, pave neighborhoods with excrement, eat the seeds for winter wheat. But above Rome, in winter, they assemble in flocks ten thousand strong and put on shows that take my breath away.

Tonight there are three flocks. They stretch into quarter-mile bands, winding apart, then slowly snapping back together. In one minute they are three separate helices, a heart, a velvet funnel, two falling scarves. A flock swings closer to us, a shower of black against the blue, plunging in coordination—suddenly a thousand birds turn their wing tips to us and are gone.

Here on the Janiculum the ancients typically posted an augur or two, priests who would interpret auspices— the flights of birds, for the most part—to determine the will of the gods. The birds swing east and it's time to go to battle. See too many hawks, or not enough, and an inauguration should be postponed. From the little I've read, leaning against a table in the Academy library, Livy's history of Rome is stuffed with good and bad auspices, generals pausing to take them, emperors ignoring them at their peril. Pliny's writing, too, is infused with omens: he claimed that ravens understood the meanings they conveyed in auspices. Eagle-owls signified direful portents, and fighting cocks gave the most powerful signs; the manner in which they ate grain determined if state officers could open their homes, and what formations soldiers would take on battlefields. These chickens, Pliny says, held "supreme empire over the empire of the world."

Down in Trastevere streetlights come on, one after another. The starlings rematerialize, washed in blue, a five-hundred-foot-tall dancer turning flips. I prop the backpack on its stand and adjust Owen's hat and give him a bottle, wondering what he sees. Maybe you know the history: In 1890, in New York City, a drug manufacturer named Eugene Schieffelin, who wanted to make sure that every bird mentioned in Shakespeare's plays was introduced to America, released eighty starlings in Central Park. A hundred and fifteen years later the United States alone has 200 million—and angry wheat farmers and flocks sucked into jet engines and histoplasmosis, a respiratory disease that originates in starling feces.

In Rome there are a million or so. When they're twirling above the rooftops, hardly anyone seems to notice. Outside the bookstore on Largo di Torre Argentina, where almost every night a flock performs arabesques above six umbrella pines, I am usually the only person on the sidewalk looking up. The few Romans who do pay attention want them gone. Volunteers torture a couple of birds, record the distress calls, then walk laps of the train station broadcasting the recordings through megaphones.

Imagine what the birds hear! Strange voices shouting, *Ouch! Ouch! Ouch!* It doesn't appear to scare them off.

In front of me, in front of Owen, ten thousand birds swerve, check up, and float. Then they plunge. A tourist at the railing asks, in English, "Who's the leader?" but no one answers. Knowingly or not, we all stand there taking our auspices, reading the omens of the birds. The real question, the one that keeps me coming back to this railing, night after night, is Why do they bother to be so beautiful?

Starling, earthling. How little we understand. Nero had a starling that spoke Greek and Latin. Mozart kept a starling in a cage beside his piano.

On the street beside me Owen hums as he drinks his milk. He explores the texture of his backpack with his fingertips; he blinks his big eyelids.

We nail a wreath to our door. We buy a two-foot-tall Douglas fir in a pot and balance it on top of the stroller and push it the mile and a half home. We eat pizza *rossa* by the kilogram; we buy shortbread cookies so rich with butter they eat through their paper bag. After a storm, a rainbow of water bottles and soccer balls gathers beneath the spillway beside Tiber Island, spinning and spinning in the foam. In the Campo dei Fiori a man pokes pigeons off the awning of his newsstand with the end of a broomstick, and the statue of the heretic Giordano Bruno, burned alive here in 1600, broods under his big bronze hood.

In Trastevere we are walking down via della Lungaretta, a long alley lined with pen and bracelet and DVD salesmen, when a man on crutches stops us. He is absorbed in the stroller; he pinches tires, examines straps. By now my replies are automatic.

"So you did not buy it here?" he asks. His foot, ankle, and shin are in a plaster cast.

I want to say, "There's always the Internet," so I try, *"Ecco sempre l'internet,"* which is more like, "Here, forever, the Internet."

"My wife," he says, "she is pregnant with twins."

"Ahhh."

He sighs, tapping one crutch against the cobbles. "And we have another daughter."

I translate for Shauna. She congratulates him.

"It is a blessing," he says. He looks past our heads, down the alley, not smiling. He seems more likely to call his broken ankle a blessing. We walk together awhile, his cast swinging back and forth between the crutches. His name is Marco. They have two bedrooms in their apartment and are not sure where they'll put the babies.

"Is it so much work?" he asks, and we laugh and say, yes, it is. *Molto lavoro.* Much work. When we reach the end of the alley, we say good-bye and he disappears into his apartment with a wave.

There is a circle of understanding, an unspoken fellowship, between parents of multiple babies. Two days ago a Roman mother grappled her twins onto the tram at Largo Argentina, one baby clipped to her chest and the other in her arms. She flipped her hair out of her face and her gaze took in Henry and Owen, the stroller, me, and for a half second our eyes met. Something in my heart flared. I thought, Hang in there. You're not alone.

By mid-December the air in the shadows has grown painfully cold. Hardly any Italians bring their children outside. In the Villa Sciarra, a children's park near the Academy, where stone fauns and nymphs stand frozen in the basins of fountains and two peacocks strut inside a chain-link aviary trailed by dozens of pigeons, we are often the only parents strolling our children.

Virgil claims in the *Aeneid* that the early Romans tossed newborns into freezing streams to "harden them," but the few baby carriages we see in winter contain infants buried in snowsuits and down comforters, not so much a baby at all as a pillow with a head and two mittens and two shoes stitched on the corners. On buses older women slide the windows shut as soon as we wheel through the doors. In the supermarket a woman in an ankle-length parka watches us bag groceries, then gestures at the boys and asks something like, "You're taking them *outside?*"

How does she think we got there? It's only forty degrees Fahrenheit, after all. Try this sometime: Park a stroller in the shade in Rome in the winter. Within a minute an Italian mother will stop. "They must be put in the sun," she'll say. Once a pair of ladies took the stroller out of my hands and wheeled it thirty feet across a piazza and positioned it themselves.

Either Virgil was lying or the Romans have gotten soft. We dress the boys in hooded sweatshirts, fleece jumpers. We draw glances of horror. We are parenting daredevils.

A week before Christmas we leave the babies with Tacy. Shauna wants to play "bus golf," climbing on and off public buses at random. A man inks detailed caricatures of John Malkovich outside a restaurant. A department store sells only garments for nuns and priests, embroidered chasubles, purple stoles, nun raincoats, nun luggage. A bak-

ery on via della Luce in Trastevere is a holy land of cookies, cookies on trays, cookies in cases, cookies piled on
plates.

A bus pulls up and Shauna drags me onto it; we ride it
two stops and she drags me off. We nibble chocolate bars
in various transepts. In the florid, late Renaissance church
of the Gesù, a jumpsuited repairman climbs into the
organist's nest and shines his flashlight across soaring
clusters of pipes. On via Giulia, a long, straight avenue
jammed with antique shops, a very old man with eggshell
skin fiddles with his window-front crèche for fifteen
minutes, repositioning shepherds and sheep, adjusting a
miniature waterwheel.

Around dusk, we drift off a busy street into an open
courtyard and pass through another open door into the
most amazing church I have ever seen.

You notice first how white it is. A few railings are
touched with gold, but all the rest is white: white six-
pointed stars, white windows, white balconies. And you
notice how unlocked it feels, free of pillars and registries
and choir stalls and auxiliary chapels. Strands of sunlight
lean through two of six high windows. It seems less a
church than a tabernacle, less a temple to God than a temple to light.

The floor plan is two equilateral triangles, one super-
imposed on top of each other, a Star of David with the
lines blown inward. As the walls rise, the segments of the
triangles produce a series of elaborate convexities and con-
cavities. I feel dizzy, I brace myself against the back of a
pew. We are enfolded in the creamy white interior of a
stomach, staring up and up into a tightening throat.

Our guidebook says it is called Sant'Ivo alla Sapienza.

By Borromini. Which makes sense, as it is clearly related to Saint Charles at the Four Fountains. I read its little paragraph aloud. Completed in 1660. The interior is stucco. The dome is inspired by earlier depictions of the tower of Babel.

"That's all?" Shauna asks.

"That's all."

She blinks. "It deserves four hundred pages."

We sit in a corner and try counting the six points of the star as the architecture climbs toward the lantern, but we quickly get dizzy and lose count; we are honeycombed, we are trapped inside the molecules at the center of a snow crystal. The pews, the crucifix, the dwarfed altar— they all seem completely irrelevant. It is all space, all geometry, all ceiling. In the restless walls I glimpse patterns: mountains and streams, snow blowing across a freeway, a train of climbers winding along the edge of a glacier. Everything forms and re-forms. We sit on our little bench and feel the church coil and twist above us, a wintry heart, a tornado of plaster.

Night falls. We walk out woozy. In the bus windows, on the way home, all we can see are the reflections of our own pale, startled faces.

Dust settles over the notes for my novel. I send off a book review for the *Boston Globe* and sit in the Academy library and feel the suction of Rome, its restlessness, its dreams. I start a journal entry about Sant'Ivo, thinking I'll spend ten minutes on it, explain the church to a notebook, then go up to the studio and start in on some fiction. Four hours later I'm still in the library, reading about construction projects in the seventeenth century. Borromini's patrons were so doubtful that the spiraling lantern atop Sant'Ivo would stay erect that he personally guaranteed the church for fifteen years. Rare stones were in such demand that architects fought over them; for centuries stonecutters had been slicing apart granite and porphyry columns salvaged from ancient buildings to use as church pavements.

Every era here, it seems, cannibalizes the previous one; everything is salvaged, recouped, reclaimed. After Nero committed suicide, the 121-foot statue of himself that he'd erected in the entrance hall of his two-hundred-acre pleasure palace soon had its head retooled to resemble succeeding emperors. The massive fourth-century triumphal arch of Constantine, still standing today near the Colosseum, consists mostly of stone and decoration plundered from monuments erected by previous emperors.

Imperial Romans took culture from the Greeks, infrastructure from the Etruscans, obelisks from the Africans. The Vandals in AD 455 stripped the Roman temple of Jupiter of all its bronze and used it to adorn the palace of their king. In AD 663, the Byzantine emperor Constans II tore the gilded roof tiles off the Pantheon and shipped them back to his own residence in Constantinople. Renaissance architects used ancient Roman supports to rebuild aqueducts and dug up imperial travertine for their churches. In one day in 1452, more than two and a half thousand cartloads of rock were supposedly pried out of the Colosseum and carted over to the construction site at St. Peter's. Meet the new temples, same as the old temples.

The bronze gilding on the Pantheon's portico outlasted the roof tiles by 950 years until, in 1625, Pope Urban VIII melted it down to cast the Baldacchino above

St. Peter's altar. With what was left over, he allegedly made eighty cannons.

The marble on the façade of the Fontanone, just down the hill from where we live, came from the Temple of Minerva in the Forum, the eighteen-hundred-year-old columns hauled up the Janiculum, the slabs sawed apart, refashioned, and reset. Bernini took columns from the fourth-century Baths of Diocletian to use in the bell towers in front of St. Peter's in 1638; they were taken out eight years later, when the half-finished towers were demolished.

This city swirls with stories—the deeper into the library stacks you go, the more stories spiral up around you. One pope's nephew beats another pope's nephew at cards in 1485 and the winnings finance the construction of the Cancelleria, a three-story palace just off the Campo dei Fiori that is the size of a city block. Can this possibly be true? Does it matter?

Here's something you can spend a day considering: At least 220 plaster flowers the size of patio tables hang from the underside of Michelangelo's cornice of the Palazzo Farnese, staring down at whoever cares to look up. Not one of these flowers is the same as any other. How long would something like that take?

Here's something else: most of the ancient temples, monuments, and statues here were originally *painted*. The color of classical Rome was not chalky white but electric blue, strawberry blond, sunshine yellow: a seven-year-old's coloring book, magenta temples, violet skies. An exhibit at the Vatican called "The Colors of White" displays a stone lion as its sculptor supposedly intended: cobalt mane, pink nails, green irises. See a bust of Caligula with hazel eyes and coral lipstick; see Venus de Milo with eye shadow and crimson nostrils. Think of it—the frieze entwined around Trajan's Column used to be a 650-foot spectrum of maroons and golds: each foot-high soldier, each tree trunk, each legionary ship, all the way up to the top, carefully colored in.

Rumor is, St. Peter isn't buried beneath the Vatican after all, but on the Janiculum. Or in Jerusalem. Rumor is, the biggest obelisk of all—a fourteenth obelisk—is buried somewhere beneath the Pantheon.

I see too little, know too little. I will never know a tenth of it. A scholar could spend a decade studying Rome's weather vanes, another studying archways, a third studying baptistery doors. And how far would she get?

Three months ago I climbed off an airplane into Rome in 2004 with a novel I thought I could write. Now where am I? And when? I blink, I breathe; the spines of the books around me seethe and rustle, each a chronicle of someone's mind, a brain that has washed into this city like a wave and broken itself against it.

Tacy looks after the babies; Shauna and I spend an evening Christmas shopping. On the walk home it is raining in St. Peter's Square and we duck into the basilica to warm up. The pews are full and a crush of young people crowds the center aisle, students, perhaps. They hold up cell phones, cameras. Flashbulbs snap. A pewter crucifix on a pole floats past their heads, making for the altar.

Near the back of the crowd I set down our shopping bags and lift Shauna by her hips. She narrates: It's a procession. First come a half dozen Swiss guards in their mustard and blue, then some men in suits, then cardinals in scarlet. The crowd presses in behind us, whispering, clicking. *"È qui,"* they say. He's here.

A couple years ago Shauna's mother and I were walking down Thirty-seventh Street in New York, on our way to a book reading, when Denzel Washington stepped out of a building and stopped maybe five feet in front of us. Across the street, behind a cordon, a group of women started screaming, "Denzel! Denzel!" Denzel looked up, waved. For a minute or so he consulted a sheet of paper while someone knelt and fed a wire up the back of his jacket. A camera rested on a crane nearby, folded like a sleeping insect; a truck hosed down the pavement. We had stumbled into a film shoot.

What was strange was that Denzel Washington's face was so completely familiar that I had to stop myself from clapping him on the shoulder. Denzel, it's me! How've you been?

When Pope John Paul II eventually comes down the central aisle of St. Peter's, the urge is the same. He is carried in a big upholstered chair, and everyone stretches onto their toes, and as I strain to lift Shauna even higher, I catch a one-second glimpse of the pope as he passes between two shoulders. He is twenty feet away, wrinkled and tired-looking, the stem of his neck drooping. His chin bobs against his chest. His profile is sharp and his eyes are soft. He is utterly familiar. It is a face I have seen a thousand times. More, probably. He has been pope since I was four years old. And the impulse is to announce our presence: John Paul, it's me! It's us!

Then he's out of sight. I set down Shauna. We are two in ten thousand anyway. In under a minute the pope is installed near the Baldacchino, a white figure in a chair fifty yards away, and someone has begun speaking into a microphone in breakneck Italian, and we go back out into the rain.

The winter solstice is Shauna's birthday. I take the morning off and we eat croissants and walk to an Egyptian glass shop near the Campo dei Fiori a friend has told Shauna about—warren after warren of dusty glassware, greens, blues, yellows, pitchers and platters and chandeliers and whole dungeons of ashtrays. The ceilings are low; the bricks brown with creosote. The shelving appears to be held together with hundred-year-old nails, and there is the occasional crash from somewhere in the basement. We buy a hundred glass flowers at a few cents apiece to string on leather and hang in the branches of our tiny Christmas tree.

In the glamorous shops northeast of there, along via Condotti, little lighted shrubs stand on red carpets. Chocolate cakes and glittering pastries sit on lace inside illuminated vitrines. Louis Vuitton wants €3,900 for a handbag; Hermès is asking €9,100 for a leather coat. We wander up to the Piazza del Popolo, where we watch two elderly ladies, totaling maybe 160 pounds, lean on a railing and dispatch cones of gelato the size of tennis-ball cans. A boy pedals his tricycle while his father pulls him along with the crook of an umbrella handle hooked around the handlebars. Accordions play, and the smell outside a café is of baking bread, dead shellfish, and spilled beer.

To live here is to live partly in a world of fantasy—the

twisting lanes, the slumbering statues, the winter sun small and cold behind the swaying heads of the pines.

On Christmas Eve we carry the babies up the stairs of the Academy and sit with them on the floor of the big living room. The moisture in their eyes reflects the slowly flashing lights of the Academy's Christmas tree. Most of the scholars and artists have returned to the States for the holidays and the whole building is quiet, devoid of even ghosts, no footfalls, no voices behind doors, no shutters ratcheting up. The library is padlocked; the studios are shut. Indeed, the entire Janiculum seems to be asleep behind the drizzle, a few lights wavering behind hedges, raindrops sliding down the panes.

We fight the boys into the stroller and fight the stroller down the stairs and walk Trastevere in the mist. Only derelicts are out, it seems, a Gypsy girl moaning on the steps of a church, pretending to be lame; a drunk staggering behind us, asking where we come from. ("Finland!" I tell him.) Lights burn behind shutters. Henry sings softly to himself.

In a church near viale Trastevere we park the boys beside a font of holy water and stand in our raincoats through the last half of a mass. Communion, a wafer dipped in sweet wine, is placed directly in my mouth. Off to my left, a plaster statute of Mary glows beneath a cheap-looking crown. As I shuffle back toward the rear of the church, pews ticking past on my right, votives burning on my left, Owen sees me from the stroller and breaks into a smile, and it sets a little bell ringing in my heart.

Mass ends, the lights come on, and thirty or so old

women file out, smiling one after another at the twins. *Che carini. Che belli.*

Periodically, while Shauna was pregnant, a nurse would show us our sons on an ultrasound screen. A hand or two, the pressed ovals of the skulls, squashed limbs washing back and forth behind blizzards of pixels—it was as if we were peering at bizarre life-forms deep under the ocean. It seemed plain they would not be entirely human: they had fish feet, dark hollows for eyes. After two years of failing to get Shauna pregnant, I'd grown accustomed to thinking parenthood happened to other people, luckier people. I had never really believed it would work the way it was supposed to, not even after Shauna's pregnancy tests came back positive; or after her twenty-week appointment when we saw the creature that would be named Henry lounging inside his amnion with his ankles crossed, Owen twisting in his own sac nearby; or even after Shauna was confined to bed and we were using phrases like *pelvic floor* and *mucus plug* in daily conversation.

Now—it has happened in an instant—the babies are nine months old and it's our first Christmas as a family. And what amazes me, day after day, is that our sons are perfectly whole. I wait for them to transform back into undersea monsters; I wait for someone to come and take one of them away.

Tonight they do a sort of belly-crawl down the hallway like soldiers creeping beneath razor wire. Their eyes glitter. Their mouths gape with concentration.

Before bed, we lower them into the tub and pour cups of water over their heads. Their little diaphragms rise and fall beneath their ribs. They lean forward in their little plastic bath chairs and slap the surface of the water and crack each other up. Shauna looks over at me and says, "We have *two children*."

Christmas morning: more rain. The four of us sit on a blanket beside our little ragged Christmas tree with its glass flowers and spill of gifts. Gifts for the boys, gifts from the States. The Italian ones are easy to find: wrapped gloriously. The Italians could wrap a used textbook and make it look like gold and frankincense.

My sister-in-law has sent homemade chocolate chip cookies, which reputedly are available in Rome, at a bakery in the Jewish quarter, but both times we have gone there it has been closed. I eat fifteen of them.

My publisher has sent me Harold McGee's *On Food and Cooking,* and I spend the afternoon reading about mushrooms, how the stems and caps we eat are only fractions of the real organism. The vast percentage of any mushroom, it turns out, lives underground, in a network of extremely fine fibers, or hyphae, that prowl the soil gathering nutrients. A single cubic centimeter of dirt might contain as much as two thousand meters of hyphae.

Rome is like that, I think. The bulk of it lies underground, its history ramified so densely under there, ten centuries in every thimbleful, that no one will ever unravel it all.

By dinnertime rain is smashing into the shutters. The thunder is soft enough that we're not quite sure it's thunder at all. We eat pork and tomatoes with mozzarella. Owen rolls off his blanket, brings his knees up under his chest, and crawls across the kitchen floor, one hand, two hands, one knee, two knees, as if he has been crawling all his life. "My God," Shauna says, and drops her fork. He looks up at us, grinning.

We give them baths. We set them in their cribs. Owen rolls over and over, a little hurricane, throwing himself against the slats.

Maybe being a new parent is like moving to a foreign country. There is a Before and an After, an Old Life and a New Life. Sometimes we wonder who we were before. Sometimes we wonder who we are now. Sometimes our feet get tired. Sometimes we find ourselves reaching for guidebooks.

We are humbled over and over—humility hangs over our heads like a sledgehammer. Oh, your novel got a nice review? That's great. You can read it after you scrub the feces out of your child's pajamas. Oh, you think you've been here long enough to barter at the street markets? Guess what, you just spent €8 on three plastic clothes hangers.

Every few days there are moments of excruciating beauty. We are simultaneously more happy and more worn out than we have ever been in our lives. We communicate by grinning and pointing and waving food in the air. We don't sleep as well as we used to. Our expectations (today I might take a shower; the #75 bus might actually show up) are routinely dashed. Just when we think we have a system (two naps a day; Shauna finds a *rosticceria* with chickens on spits that is open on Sundays), the system collapses. Just when we think we know our way around, we get lost. Just when we think we know what's coming next, everything changes.

On the day after Christmas all four of us wake up ravaged by viruses. A deepwater pressure pounds in the space behind my nose, and pain drags through the bottoms of my eyes. Shauna can barely get out of bed. Henry stares glumly into space. Owen has it the worst. He sits on his mat and coughs like an old smoker. Twin cascades of phlegm stream down his upper lip. The coughs come in threes and he lowers his head and rakes the mitts of his hands across his face.

It feels as if we have been locked in a trunk that is slowly sinking toward the sea bottom. Shauna measures medicine into droppers. I switch on the computer and read that an earthquake in Sri Lanka has killed two thousand people. Fifteen minutes later CNN says the earthquake was in India and Thailand and has killed five thousand. Then ten thousand.

We drink foul-tasting Italian cough syrup. In the afternoon I fall asleep and have several consecutive nightmares that I will accidentally kill the boys. I bring Henry into the building, grappling with too many sacks of groceries, and drop him on the stairs. Owen rolls off the sawhorses and plank we use as a diaper table and crashes into the bathtub. I hold Henry on the terrace and he plummets off; I hold Owen in the window to show him a bird and he falls out.

I wake shivering. By dinnertime, the earthquake's toll is up to twenty-five thousand and the Vatican radio station is calling it a tsunami. *Tsunami:* Japanese for "harbor wave."

That night we hardly sleep. We are hot, we are cold. Sweat gathers in our clothes. We wipe our noses; we lie in the darkness with trees growing in our foreheads.

Somewhere in Iraq a British army sergeant is killed. Somewhere on the white beaches of Indonesia a thousand bodies start to rot. Around two in the morning I check on Owen in his crib. He is wide awake, not crying. His hair is stringy and clings to his forehead. When I change his diaper, his chest is pale, his forearms cool. His temperature is 102 degrees Fahrenheit. In the morning he starts coughing and does not let up, sets of three coughs followed by cries. We rush him around the apartment, showing him various toys, trying to get the fit to stop. For twenty-five minutes he does not stop coughing except to inhale. Eventually Shauna unplugs the telephone and lets him poke the buttons, which calms him for a moment. He sits over the phone, his torso rocking gently back and forth. I can hear him breathing from across the room.

"It's just a cough," I tell Shauna. "Just a fever."

But how do we know, for sure, that he is not trapped in the fist of a fatal illness? All of a sudden, it seems, the shadow of apocalypse has crept across everything. The tsunami death toll climbs like a deficit counter: eighty thousand, ninety thousand. I can't take my eyes off the computer screen: trees stuffed through rooftops, orphans weeping in tents. A hotel restaurant fills with brown water. A floating log, draped in fabric, sweeps backward between buildings.

"Shut it off," Shauna says. "That's enough."

I watch it again. The log is not a log. It is not a log.

A giant basaltic plate, grinding across the surface of the earth at a speed roughly comparable to the rate at which our fingernails grow, smashes into another plate, and the resulting percussion sends waves to drown a hundred thousand people.

A hundred thousand. Half the population of Boise. Is that everybody I know? Everybody I've ever met? Even one hundred thousand is too big to fully understand.

The pediatrician rides a Vespa. "All of Rome is sick," he says, and washes his hands in our sink for three minutes. He says the boys need rest, hot steam, more cough syrup. Before he leaves, he asks if he can borrow a tissue.

Owen sits dazed on his mother's lap, medicine working on him, virus working on him, all his shining, young cells fighting. I go to the studio and open a notebook and write, *Wind rattles the pane. Are you afraid?* That's as far as I get. I spend the rest of the morning watching video clips of devastated villages. The death toll passes 150,000.

Here lies One Whose Name was writ in Water. And another. And another.

Rain taps the window. Is this what it's like living in the twenty-first century? My friend Al writes, "Start gathering animals. I'll prepare the ark." I think, I should start keeping an ax in the corner of the bedroom.

To see our planet from space, you'd never know about all our human dramas, all these desperations being played out in our deserts and forests and wetlands, the earth a tinderbox of sage and cheatgrass, thirty tectonic plates floating atop an asthenosphere of half-melted asphalt. The bright flares of human desires, the endless, unsympathetic swirling of oblivion. Here's another duality of Rome: the way time here feels simultaneously immense and tiny.

One day we are positively huge, at center stage. The next we are a snowflake, falling through the clouds, circling, dropping through the hole in the roof of a temple, alighting on the floor, and vanishing.

If the 4.5 billion years the earth has existed were represented by a soccer field, the hundred thousand years of human history since agriculture would be represented by an endline one-hundredth of an inch across—a margin no thicker than a blade of grass.

Fate is whimsy: I could be you, reading this page; you could be on a breakwater in Sri Lanka, or making dinner in your house in Pompeii, laughing with your daughter, five minutes left to live. Everywhere the world reminds us how little control we have, the wind tearing through your jacket, a little cluster of bacteria hiding in your hamburger.

To walk out a door or inhale or tie a shoe is to risk your life. You stoop; an invisible, silent bullet might just whiz past your head, or it might fly straight through your throat. Pliny and the ancients, with their circuses and mock naval battles and a first-century population with as many slaves as citizens seemed to understand this better than we do. Even the emperors, many of whom fancied themselves gods, could be made away with as cheaply as anybody else: a coughing fit, a plate of toxic mushrooms, a knife in the back.

On August 24, AD 79, Pliny the Elder was south of Rome, in the Bay of Naples, when smoke started rising from Vesuvius. He asked that ships be made ready and sailed for Stabiae, a seaside resort town near Pompeii. "Was he afraid?" wondered his nephew. "It seems not, as he kept up a continuous observation of the various movements and shapes of that evil cloud, dictating what he saw."

The wind carried Pliny across the bay. Ash and pumice rained onto the decks. He made notes; he speculated on causes for the eruption. In Stabiae, he met with leaders, even took a bath. The buildings were shaking; ash billowed into the streets. He helped escort evacuees to the shore, but the sea had risen, and the wind had trapped their boats. According to his nephew, Pliny took refuge in the shade of a sail, asked for some cool water, and asphyxiated as two slaves tried to help him up.

It's hard not to think of Pliny's nephew, seventeen years old, back at Misenum, staring across the bay, wondering about the fate of his uncle. The distant ash, the blue sky beyond. What's the difference, I wonder, between those of us who sit and watch, and those of us who sail across the bay? Can curiosity be a form of courage?

"As a protection against falling objects they put pillows on their heads tied down with cloths," Pliny's nephew wrote. "Elsewhere there was daylight by this time, but they were still in darkness, blacker and denser than any ordinary night."

On New Year's Eve I drink beer with some of the other fellows on the roof of the Academy. Shauna is still sick, the boys are finally recovering, sleeping in their cribs, and I have not added more than a few new pages to my war novel in weeks. The moon rises over the Alban Hills huge and lopsided and red. Ten minutes before midnight, fireworks begin streaking into the sky from every neighborhood, the historic center, Trastevere, the suburbs, the Castelli Romani in the distant hills—little flowers of green and red, a thousand muted booms. January: month of Janus, Roman god of gates and archways, god of transitions, god of middle grounds. He watches over the borderland between country and city, watches over harvests and births; he is the mascot of the American Academy, and the Janiculum is named for him.

Somewhere in Indonesia cars are still trapped in trees and people sleep stupefied in debris, and here in Rome spent rockets are kicked to the gutters and Peter Pan flies through the Piazza del Popolo and the shadows of figures walk the Janiculum in front of the Academy, holding hands, peering up at us, then down at the city.

On the way home I pause on the front stairs. A carving of Janus presides over the Academy's entrance, one face on the front of his head and another on the back. Above the roofline, the undersides of the clouds flash copper. To my right is Jon Piasecki's studio, bristling with carved stumps and painted branches and stones with holes drilled in them. To my left is George Stoll's studio, impeccably clean, all white, a half dozen fastidiously polished plaster bowls sitting on tables.

Ten feet above me, Janus peers at George's studio and Jon's, at Trastevere and the Vatican, at the past and the future. More dialectics; more sets of twins.

Lorenzo is gone for the night. I have to clamber over the six-foot wall beside the front gate to get home. The sparks of a firework drift slowly down over the pines.

I hate seeing my kids sick. When you've never seen them recover before, you're not quite convinced they can do it.

On the fourth of January my second book comes out in the UK and my publisher flies me to London. The Alps drift along far below—shining with snow, creased every-where. In the lavatory the tissues are labeled *Tissues* and the flusher says *Press here to flush*. The flight attendant greets me with a *"Buongiorno,"* then asks, in perfect English, "What would you like to drink?"

Rather than feel comforted, I am disappointed. It is the same chagrin I feel when I overhear American tourists in Rome say something like "Oh, I've been to St. Kitts." I am one of them, hardly more than a tourist myself, but to go to London and be spoken to in English, to be able to eaves-drop on conversations again, after a season and a half of being surrounded by Italian, feels like cheating. As if life should not be so automatic, as if we Americans ought always to be reminded of this.

Shauna will be putting the twins down for their morn-ing nap by now. I think of Owen belly-crawling this morning on the wooden floor of the Academy's living room, Shauna and I sitting on the antique trunk outside the bar, sipping latte *macchiati,* Owen's small body sliding across the wood, his palms dragging him to a dropped spoon, the fireplace, his mother's shoelace. He runs his fin-gers over the carved face of the trunk; he shrieks in delight.

"A second birth," Maria Montessori called it, when a child can move away from his mother on his own. And indeed Owen does seem like a new child, rarely crying, constantly at work on getting himself somewhere else.

Now the slow shaking of another 767, the big, dead television monitors, the flight attendants plying their carts. France is consumed in white vapor. The sky floats away.

I return fifty hours later. Monteverde is busy and dark. There's the newsstand, the pizzeria, the corner bar, son at the cappuccino machine, father at the register, both wearing paper hats. They whisk past: there, then gone. It is strange to race in the back of a taxi through these fifteen or so blocks, the confines of our daily life—which I have known before now only on foot—in under a minute.

I run up the stairs into the apartment but everybody is asleep. I peek in at Henry and Owen, then bring a cup of tea onto the terrace. There are a few stars. My breath drifts away in white clouds. How urbane and modern London seemed, with its pale faces and straight avenues and fast food and *cheers*es and *pardon*s and *loo*s. London is old, of course, but coming from Rome it felt refurbished and youthful; it was not so burdened with cracking and crumbling, not so dusky and battered. Starbucks and KFC glowed on street corners. All the menus were in English, all the signs intelligible. But here? In Rome I could live twenty years and never be sure I hadn't missed some hugely important, tree-lined avenue ten blocks from our apartment. It is the puzzle of Rome that mesmerizes: its patience, its stratigraphy, Tiber mud gumming up the past, wind carrying dust from Africa, rain pulling down ruins, and the accumulated weight of centuries compacting everything tighter, transubstantiating all stones into one.

Tonight, for some reason my brain can almost fit itself around the fact that the universe is expanding, time and space blowing outward, our galaxy swirling wider and wider, the faint starlight shining on this terrace older than the founders of Rome, older than the dinosaurs, traveling from stars some of which have long since collapsed and exploded, leaving behind carbon shells, smoldering and impossibly heavy.

And yet there they are, gleaming away, signal lights shining out of the past.

Days of scarves and parkas. Days of too many items in too many pockets—one bottle of milk in one back pocket, another in the other. Pen, wallet, phrase book, keys; a blanket for the boys over a shoulder; notepad and money clip; the baby carrier strapped over my chest with Henry inside; Owen wriggling in my left arm, his fingers in my hair, chin hauling back—he becomes an angry wolverine. A stamped letter for the postbox is clamped in my teeth. A recycling bag jammed full of paper hangs from one wrist. Do I have a pacifier? Rain shield for the stroller?

In the States, practically every time someone would stop us on the street or in the grocery store, they'd gesture at the stroller and say, "Twins? Bet you have your hands full." They'd mean well, of course, but to be reminded of something you can't forget is debilitating. I prefer the Italian mothers who lean over the stroller and whisper, "So beautiful," the smiles of passing children, the old Roman who stopped us today and grinned at Henry and Owen before shaking my hand and saying, with a bow, *"Complimenti."* My compliments.

In the middle of January, Shauna's mother flies to Rome. The second morning she is here, she agrees to come over from her hotel at 7 a.m. and watch the babies. Shauna and

I bolt down grapefruit juice, ride the #115 bus to St. Peter's, and walk through the big, empty piazza, everything wet with rain, the fountains splashing, the façade of the basilica gray and damp.

We thread along the Vatican walls and enter a section of the city we haven't seen before. Shops hawk pope-shaped lollipops and plastic Virgins; a bakery sells pastries shaped like papal miters.

We are in line for the Vatican Museums before 8. Twenty minutes later the umbrellas in front of us are shuffling forward, and we pick a lucky metal detector and a lucky ticket booth, passing a few tour groups as they gather in bleary-eyed clusters, and we slip through an archway and break into a run down a mile-long hallway with a somber courtyard unscrolling endlessly beyond the left-hand windows, tapestries sailing past, the 130-yard-long Hall of Maps sailing past, the Hall of Masks, the Hall of Muses, the various guards watching us bemusedly, and soon there is no one in front of us at all, only gallery after gallery, and the taciturn exteriors of Vatican buildings advancing beyond the windows. After three or so more minutes of jogging, we come breathless past the Raphael Rooms to a final staircase and a cluster of six or seven guards, most of them on cell phones, and step down into the Sistine Chapel alone.

It's darker than I thought it would be, and rawer, and older. It smells like musty newspapers.

Four years of work, eight-hour days, lying on his back. In the quiet we imagine him, big-eared, broken-nosed, left-handed Michelangelo, young when he did the ceiling, old when he did the back wall, walking here on a drizzly morning like this one, limping down the halls in his dogskin boots, the day's plaster wet and waiting, the vault silent. You take a breath, you go back to work.

For five minutes Shauna and I are the only people in the Sistine Chapel. Eventually another couple arrives, out of breath. A tour group enters through a door I hadn't even noticed. Still, there are less than twenty of us. Shauna and I lie on a bench beneath the Drunkenness of Noah and whisper.

The ceiling sets our heads fully on the stem of our necks, our eyes in their sockets. I will remember, more than anything else, the feet of Jonah, fifty feet up, muscular and arched, dangling above the Last Judgment, his torso contorted in his throne, his expression seemingly in awe both of the miracle of his own existence and of the ceiling laid out above him.

You find your way through a place by getting lost in it. Winter in Rome is a breath of daylight, then limestone and shadow: light glowing behind closed shutters as though stacks of gold are hoarded inside. In a window in Campo Marzio, not far from Augustus's sundial, two thousand silk neckties, each in its own cubbyhole, shine like tropical birds. In San Lorenzo, east of the train station, we drink hot chocolate thick as oil. At the Holy Staircase, a half mile from the Colosseum, where Christian pilgrims are supposed to ascend twenty-eight marble steps on their knees, we see a man furtively tuck a folded newspaper beneath his shins as he climbs.

Rivers of cars circulate through the city, dashing along here, stalling in eddies there. Shauna pulls another tissue from her purse. To spend a day walking the streets in

Rome, we're told, is to inhale the equivalent of eighteen cigarettes.

I push the twins to the vegetable market in the morning and a woman passes, smoking. Two more pass, smoking. A man in a business suit revs his dirt bike—complete with shocks and knobby tires—at a stoplight.

No wonder the pope has been shuttling in and out of the hospital. I think of Henry and Owen's ten-month-old bronchi, bright and pink; I think of John Paul's trachea, eighty-four years of Polish and Italian pollution worn into its rings.

In St. Peter's Square, reporters smoke and aim cameras at pilgrims: *Are you praying for His Holiness?*

Am I? When the breeze is down and the light is right, you can stand on the lip of the Janiculum and see the smog: ribbons of blue and gold draped above the churches.

Here, from the newspaper, is the latest antipollution measure:

> The city of Rome will limit driving within the *fascia verde* on Thursdays to cars with either odd or even license plates. Starting Jan. 13, if your car has an even license plate number, you will not be able to drive between the hours of 9 a.m. and noon and again from 3 to 7 p.m. The following Thursday it will be the turn of the odd numbers. And so on, alternating between odd and even through March 31.

The regulations are so convoluted and maddening they become almost beautiful. Which is what it's like here. We've lived in Rome four months now and I still do not understand when I am supposed to pay for coffee at a bar.

Or try this. Ten years ago a plaster Madonna in a garden in Civitavecchia, a village north of the city, cried tears of blood. Last week, a report released by "a team of legal, medical, religious, and scientific experts" was printed in the paper, concluding that the event "was supernatural as there is no scientific explanation for the tears."

Rome is a broken mirror, the falling strap of a dress, a puzzle of astonishing complexity. It is an iceberg floating below our terrace, all its ballast hidden beneath the surface.

A man passes in a suit, fur-covered boots, and mirrored sunglasses. A little boy passes wearing a watchcap printed *Versace*. A woman brushes my shoulder, her gloved hands clutching sheet music, Mozart's name across the top. This is the city where Renaissance bankers served soup made from parrot tongues. This is the city where the ancient Etruscans may or may not have had thousand-member orgies, and vestal virgins found "guilty" of intercourse were entombed alive with enough food that they wouldn't die right away, and spectators at beheadings would wager on the number of spurts of blood that would gush from a headless body.

Crucifixions, stake-burnings, entrails cranked out by mobs. In *Roman History,* the second-century senator and historian Cassius Dio describes a wealthy Roman named Vedius Pollio, who kept big saltwater reservoirs stocked with moray eels "that had been trained to eat men, and he was accustomed to throw to them such of his slaves as he desired to put to death." In Trastevere, Saint Cecilia was scalded by steam for three days in AD 230 before finally having her head hacked off. Saint George was torn up by giant gearworks a century later and forced to wear red-hot shoes, and still he wouldn't die. Thirteen hundred years after that, a governor of Cesare Borgia's held his page over a fire with a poker. One pope started forcing Jews to race down the Corso in front of horses, and another nailed the ears of heretics to doors. And what was heresy, really? A poorly timed question? Aiming a lens at a star?

We arrange, over the Internet, to rent a farmhouse for a week near an Umbrian town called Todi, two hours north. We arrange to rent a minivan called a Picasso. The minivan costs almost as much as the house. To secure it, I have to sign seven different forms. I drive it to the apartment slowly, horns following me all the way.

The stroller. Diapers, wipes, high chairs, two car seats. Two grocery bags loaded with baby food in jars. Winter jumpers, overalls, a stack of little fleece pajamas. Our last bag, containing Shauna's and my clothes, is an afterthought. As we pull past the Academy, on our way out of town, Lorenzo hurries out of the gatekeeper's shed.

"You are driving?" He peers into the backseat at the babies. He adjusts his glasses. "You have done this before?"

"Since I was sixteen."

His expression is serious, earnest. He is, I decide, one of the most considerate men I have ever met. "Romans don't use turn signals," he says.

We creep through Monteverde. Cars and vans blast past on both sides. Soon we are in the new Rome, billboards and construction barrels, a Hilton, a tractor dealership, tenements in reclaimed fields, glass-and-steel towers ringed by reefs of gleaming cars. Shauna ends up discarding the map and announces exit numbers on instinct. I find the driving is easiest if I pretend I am playing a video game.

A statistic: you are fifty times more likely to die on the roads in Rome than you are in Los Angeles or London. Romans are famous for their adoration of children, and yet, if you stand on a sidewalk for, say, three minutes, chances are two helmetless fourteen-year-olds will tear past you on a Vespa.

The Picasso fares admirably: one U-turn, no accidents. The sprawl dissipates. Vineyards climb the shaggy hills. Little stands of oak here and there cling to their leaves. Olive groves groove the hillsides; a commuter train pours through a tunnel. A BMW hurtles past us, going maybe 130 miles an hour. The boys scatter Cheerios across the backseat, singing, "Ma, ma, ma, ma."

Our rental is a stone farmhouse on three acres. It's near dark when we arrive. We fill an upstairs tub with brown water and bathe Owen and Henry and set them to sleep in cribs from which Shauna has painstakingly removed mouse droppings.

Out the windows the Milky Way is dazzling and white. The house feels enormous to us, creaky as a freighter, full of big rooms and old furniture. I have forgotten what it is like to live in a space like this, with a real oven and loaded bookshelves, stacks of pillows and blankets, two dining tables, a kitchen island, windowsills, three fireplaces. I have forgotten what it is like to be surrounded by quiet.

We climb into a soft bed. Pale curtains drift around us. It is so silent I can hear the branches of the trees outside the window clicking softly against each other.

"I want a house," Shauna says.

Umbria in January is smoky and blue. The rosebushes are bare. Dead leaves rattle in the dwarf oaks, and olive cuttings litter the groves.

An hour after dawn it begins to snow. It tinkles on the branches and the woodpile like shavings of glass. The valley below the house is a brilliant white; three soft lights glow far below us. The sun comes up and sets the hills on fire. After breakfast we barricade the boys into the living room with pillows and blankets; we hide lamp cords and fireplace tools. They are not walking yet, but by now both can crawl at what seems like twenty miles an hour. They pull themselves up on chairs; they crash through our puny fortifications like runaway trucks. Every few minutes there is a sickening thud as something heavy is pulled over, followed by a long inhalation, the pause as you run toward them when you think, Maybe this time he won't cry. Then there's the screaming.

We eat roast chicken, roast potatoes, pork loin, apple pie. It is the first time we have used an oven since we arrived in Italy.

Out here in Umbria, perhaps even more so than in Rome, you begin to get a sense of how long Italy has been home to humans. Everywhere we walk there are centuries-old groves and sleep-soaked farmhouses and ruins of walls: I feel as though we might start memories up from the fields as we might startle bevies of quail back home. But I feel, too, that this Italy is not quite known yet, either, not completely subdued. Time is larger here. Hawks come over the house and frost whitens the mulberries and the earth coughs up luminous, round pebbles of quartz. Mud sucks at our boots. The Tiber flows along at the bottom of the road, brown and fast, its shallows glazed with ice.

An unexpected thing happens: I start writing fiction again. The image of Rome as I first saw it comes back to me, the view from the rim of the Janiculum: the Fontanone thundering behind us, the rooftops and domes and gardens of the city wavering beneath a field of blue. The panorama floats in front of my eyes, and by lunchtime I am five pages into a new short story about a village that will be drowned by the construction of a dam.

Maybe it's that Italy has become familiar enough that I can stop paying attention to it for a few hours a day. Or maybe it's just being back in the country, a place so much more similar to home, where men go for long walks in the hills and people wave to you when you drive past and the background noise is not engines but silence. Regardless, the notebook pages begin to fill with an imaginary world. I work in the attic on a desk covered with the dead husks of wasps, legs turned up, writing out new pages, one after the other. Shauna reads in an armchair beside the fire. The boys nap hard, curled into the corners of their cribs. The sky is silver all week.

Toward the end of January my recently published novel comes out in the Netherlands and I climb onto an airplane. One after another reporters come into an Amsterdam hotel room clutching a copy of my book in Dutch. A grandfather clock chimes the hours. Behind its face little wooden ships rock to and fro, marking the seconds.

I answer the same questions a dozen times. By the end

of the day I've had so much coffee my hands are vibrat-
ing. Amsterdam seems a city of ghosts, motionless all
evening, rain falling quietly on the canals, no horns or car
alarms, just pale, lovely people gliding through intersections on bicycles. The streets disappear into curtains of
mist. In the red-light district bored women in lingerie
stand framed behind windows the size of phone booths,
shifting their weight from hip to hip.

Five years ago this was a future I wouldn't have
believed in: that good-looking European strangers would
have read my books, that in a single day I'd see my face
reflected in the lenses of fifteen different cameras. Canals
and fresh fish with my Dutch editor and a box of exquis-
ite chocolates in my room with a note from the manager
and a gorgeous Belgian newspaperwoman riding three
and a half hours on a train to come talk to me about something I made up—it's like a dream.

I walk London with Jessica the publicist; I walk Amsterdam with Esther the publicist. The flower market, the
big, black capsule of another radio microphone, a photo
shoot outside the Rijksmuseum, and tomorrow a flight
back to an apartment from the terrace of which I can see
the Pantheon—one would think it'd feel glamorous. But
it doesn't, not quite. Instead I lie in hotel beds and miss
my family. The hours when people ask me about books
I've already written feel mostly as if another person
undergoes them. It's part of a previous life; my heart is
elsewhere. This, I suppose, is what it means to look after
two babies: any attempt to make you feel as if you were at
the center of something is hopelessly hilarious.

Even now, when I have a chance to sleep all night, I
cannot. I write some new pages for my short story; I switch

on the news. During the first break, a Volvo in a commercial slips across a cypress-lined road and suddenly, impossibly, snakes past the Fontanone. The thick, bullet-shaped marble piers in front of the fountain, carved with dragons, are unmistakable.

Wet pavement, arc lights, a sleek sedan. My sons dream their own dreams just a couple hundred yards from that very spot.

I finally fall asleep around three. In a dream a single snowflake comes spiraling through the oculus of the Pantheon and lands on the floor and shines a moment before melting.

I come through the door carrying two sacks of tulip bulbs. Shauna tells me the boys have started skipping naps again. "And they scream for no reason," she says. "They're sitting there, drooling away, and suddenly they start screaming."

Constipated? Hungry? We pry open their mouths and peer in—the tissues of their gums are swollen and red. They have runny noses. They want to be held nonstop.

All week we take turns aiming brown, bad-smelling drops onto their gums, wrestling them into diapers, handing them frozen washcloths to suck on. In the mornings I mold paragraphs for my short story, examine them, try to figure out what I want to say. As soon I'm back in the apartment, I hurry Shauna out. Watching teething babies is like watching over a thermonuclear reactor—it is best done in shifts, by well-rested people.

On a dazzling and cold first day of February, Tacy watches the boys while Shauna and I walk the two and a half miles to the Piazza del Popolo. Near dusk we find ourselves on the north side of the square, in the church of Santa Maria del Popolo, standing in front of Caravaggio's *Crucifixion of Saint Peter*. It's a massive painting, dark and grainy, loaded with maroons and blacks. In it, three faceless workmen struggle to raise a solid-timber crucifix to which an aged and muscular Saint Peter has been nailed upside down.

The church smells of old wood, stone, and the ashes of incense. A restorer's drill whines on scaffolding behind us. I squint into the gloom. The painting is hung in a shadowy chapel, it's four hundred years old, and Caravaggio used so much black that it's hard to make out much of anything. I am about to move on when a man shuffles up, rifles in his pocket, and plunks a coin into a box mounted on the rail beside me. There is a click from somewhere above us and a spotlight mounted on the ceiling switches on and bathes the painting in light.

The white on Saint Peter's chest and knees springs forward; I can discern wrinkles on his forehead, grime on his ribs. A strange and alienated concern appears in his face, as if he cannot figure out where to set his gaze. In the calves and forearms of the crucifiers, there is the obvious strain of heaving up a heavy old peasant. For the first time I understand what art critics mean when they say Caravaggio was a master at using white: Peter's loincloth, centered on the canvas, bright and creased, vaults into the eye. The artist has used maybe twenty strokes of white in a vast landscape of black, but with it he has made an entire universe spring to life.

The spotlight burns for a minute, then clicks off. The painting falls back into shadow. We blink. I leave the church wondering, How many other places around here have these illumination boxes?

Light touches the frames of the windows. Ice glazes the bottom of the little blue basin we leave on the terrace for recycling. By noon the ice will be water again and it'll be warm enough to set the boys' high chairs outside.

I work every morning on the story about the flooding village. I slink into the Tom Andrews Studio with notebooks and coffee; the sky out the window is almost always dark purple. There is a feeling that dawn in Rome, in early February, is not a moment but a series of folding petals blooming outward, one after another, then falling away, while new ones, subtly lighter, take their place.

All morning I lay down sentences, erase them, and try new ones. Soon enough, when things go well, the world around me dwindles: the sky out the window, the furious calm of the big umbrella pine ten feet away, the smell of dust falling onto the hot bulb in the lamp. That's the miracle of writing, the place you try to find—when the room, your body, and even time itself cooperate in a vanishing act. Gone are the trucks rumbling outside, the sharp edge of the desk beneath my wrists, the unpaid electricity bill back in Idaho. It might seem lonesome but it's not: soon enough characters drift out of the walls, quiet and watchful, some more distinct than others, waiting to see what will happen to them. And writers come, too. Sometimes every fiction writer I've ever admired is there, from Flaubert to Melville to Wharton, all the books I've loved, all the novels I've wished I were talented enough to write. Lately Pliny leans on the edge of the desk like some old pharmacist, breathing through his nose, smelling of camphor, shaking his head every once in a while.

Sometimes, at the back of my mind, I sense the other artists in this big, drafty Academy, too, the architects and sculptors and composers asleep or just waking up, turning over their own work in their minds. I imagine them as little flames burning in their beds, flaring as the morning progresses, flames down in the library, flames in the windows of the studios, flames passing through the courtyard and out into the garden.

I x-ray sentences; I claw away a paragraph and reshape it as carefully as I can, and test it again, and peer into the pages to see if things in there are any clearer, any more resolved. Often they are not. But to write a story is to inch backward and forward along a series of planks you are cantilevering out into the darkness, plank by plank, inch by inch, and the best you can hope is that each day you find yourself a little bit farther out over the abyss.

Eventually the spell breaks. Someone turns on his shower on the other side of the wall, or I realize my hands are freezing, or my stomach is cramping, and the studio floods back in. Gravity, the smell of someone's microwaved broccoli in the kitchen down the hall, air brakes squealing somewhere beyond the garden walls, the material demands and limitations of life.

The big trunk of the umbrella pine looms outside the window, living its two lives—the upper world of needles and stems, the lower world of roots and soil. I leave the studio, shake off the dream, and go back to Shauna, the twins, Rome, that louder, more insistent dream.

❦

Carnival, *carnevale*: it comes from the Latin *carn* (flesh) and *levare* (to put away). On the Sunday before Ash Wednesday, we stroll through the Campo dei Fiori, past a bakery on via dei Baullari (the street of the trunk makers) with rows of pastries and pizzas steaming in the windows and a mortadella—a massive bologna, flecked with cubes of fat, thick as a church pillar—balanced on sawhorses beside the doorway. We cross the corso Vittorio Emanuele II and stop to watch a street vendor weave herons from palm fronds. All over Piazza Navona, children tramp and stomp, their breath showing in the cold, the masks of their costumes thrown back on their heads: Mary Poppins, Tweety Bird, homemade princesses and devils. Our shoes kick up tiny scraps of colored paper; it coats the stroller wheels. Occasionally a child flings a handful onto Henry and Owen, little stars and circles and squares. The boys are not pleased.

Only children wear costumes, and pretty much only around Piazza Navona. The parties used to be better. Here's Livy on the Bacchanalia: "When the license offered by darkness had been added, no sort of crime, no kind of immorality, was left unattempted. There were more obscenities practiced between men than between men and women. Anyone refusing to submit to outrage or reluctant to commit crimes was slaughtered as a sacrificial victim."

Here's Plutarch on Lupercalia, which had pre-Roman origins and fell on the fifteenth of February: "At this time many of the magistrates and many young men of noble families run through the city naked, and, in their jesting and merrymaking, strike those whom they meet with shaggy thongs. And many women of high rank purposely stand in their way and hold out their hands to be struck, like children at school."

The shaggy thongs were bloody strips of goat skin, which supposedly conferred fertility. The whip was called the *februa;* it gives February its name. Much later, in the eighteenth and nineteenth centuries, during Carnival, all the Romans wore costumes, from cardinals to coachmen. Banners flapped from balconies; streamers, confetti, and flour poured from windows. After dark the carriages and crowds along the via del Corso would be pushed to the sides, and riderless horses, strung with ribbons, spurred on by spiked balls tied into their manes, would charge out of Piazza del Popolo and race the mile to the Piazza Venezia at the far end, trampling anyone in their way.

Goethe waded into the throngs in 1788. "At a given signal," he wrote, "everyone has leave to be as mad and foolish as he likes, and almost everything, except fisticuffs and stabbing, is permissible."

Dickens waded in fifty-seven years later: "The jingling of the [horses'] trappings, and the rattling of their hoofs upon the hard stones; the dash and fury of their speed along the echoing street; nay, the very cannon that are fired—these noises are nothing to the roaring of the multitude: their shouts: the clapping of their hands."

Carnival: a building madness, meat roasting on every fire. Then comes Ash Wednesday, the cold rinse of the Ave Maria, and for forty days the flesh gets put away.

Owen slaps his hands on the tiles as he crawls. Henry eases in behind him, both of them slipping single file under the kitchen table. Seeing them, I think of migrating animals, one wildebeest following another. Henry can clap his hands now, and Owen sings in the mornings, but wakes screaming every night at exactly 10:35 p.m. and has to be hugged and reassured.

"It's the teeth," Shauna says. Everything is the teeth.

Still, their energy is breathtaking. Trying to dress them after a bath is like trying to put pajamas on a mackerel. Every time they manage to break into our bedroom, they seize the power cord to the computer and pull as hard as they can; four times I have caught the computer before it hit the floor. All day they drive the kitchen chairs across the tile and produce the worst screeching noise imaginable. Shauna constructs a shield of cardboard and shipping tape around the power cord from our radio, but two hours later Owen has figured out how to unravel it and is sitting in the center of the kitchen with the entire plug stuffed in his mouth.

In the Villa Sciarra, the children's park with the fauns and peacocks, we set the boys on blankets and they go motoring off into the shrubs. Four or five Italian kids circle them, pat their backs, offer them lollipops. I try to relax. All I can think is, Germs.

At midnight, at one, at two, I can't sleep. I go out on the terrace in a coat and wool hat and hack apart the dirt caked into the fifteen or so pots left out there by some previous tenant. I pull out the dead weeds and break up the soil with my fingers and cram in new tulip bulbs, hardly any space between them, twenty bulbs per pot.

At two in the morning the Alban Hills are blue, threaded with lights. A couple passes below me in the street, the woman lagging behind the man. She pauses, adjusts a strap on her shoe. The orange tip of her cigarette arcs out into the night.

"Esta, mi dispiace," the man calls back. Esta, I'm sorry. She straightens, looks around. Then she laughs.

I am awake more hours than I've ever been in my life, and yet the days and nights in Rome seem to skim past like pages in a flip-book.

On the seventeenth of February, the pope returns to the hospital, suffering from headaches. Stills from a videotape of an Italian journalist, Giuliana Sgrena, kidnapped two weeks earlier in Baghdad, are printed on the front page of every Italian paper. "I beg you," she reportedly says on the tape, "put an end to the occupation. I beg . . . the Italian people to put pressure on the government to pull out." She is kneeling with her back to a blank wall and her palms are pressed together. "Please do something for me."

Soccer stars show up for practice wearing *Liberate Giuliana* T-shirts. A giant picture of her is hung from City Hall. I open the atlas in the library and realize, for the first time, that Rome is closer to Baghdad than Boise is to Washington, D.C.

What does Pope John Paul, tucked into a hospital bed, surrounded by flowers, whisper tonight into the ear of God? Does he pray for kidnapped newspaperwomen? Or for the swollen gums of little children? He probably dreams bigger: the planet gliding through space, the slow grinding of tectonic plates.

I convince myself: it will not snow in Rome this winter.

Some nights, carrying another sack of dirty diapers to the Dumpster, washing another sinkful of baby bottles, we begin to feel glutted, oversaturated. Church interiors meld from one to the next, two-thousand-year-old columns float past unnoticed. Was that another Michelangelo? Another Pinturicchio? Fifty years ago, in *Rome and a Villa,* the novelist Eleanor Clark called it the "too-muchness" of Rome, and I feel she's right as I stand at the Dumpsters and watch the vapor of my breath float away: the Fontanone is straight ahead, the fabled city below that, but all I see is sludge and broken glass. Too much beauty, too much input; if you're not careful, you can overdose.

Cook spaghetti, peel an apple. Cut spaghetti and apple into small pieces. Place on high-chair trays. Watch Henry and Owen throw food onto the floor. Pick it up off the floor. Wash high-chair trays. In the city we pass Romans reading novels, talking in the sun, happily devouring their *contorni* at a café in the Jewish quarter. They wear ironed shirts, their hair is neatly coiffed, their shoes gleam. I stare at them through the bars of parenthood. Why don't they have milk stains on their shoulders? Why do they get to sleep through the night?

If I didn't have you, Owen; if I didn't have you, Henry. If I didn't have you, I would be able to eat lunch with two hands.

Then, just when I need it, there is something like this: I am carrying Owen down the stairwell when we pass a man I've never seen before on his way up.

"Ciao," I say.

"Ciao," the man says.

"Ciao," Owen says. It is the first time he's ever said it. I almost fall over. The man grins.

"*Ciao!*" the man replies. He flourishes his cane and bows.

A line from Marilynne Robinson's *Gilead* comes back to me. "There are a thousand thousand reasons to live this life, every one of them sufficient."

One polished, windy morning, two weeks into Lent, some Academy fellows take me to the top of Mt. Testaccio. Mt. Testaccio looks like any of the other Roman hills, but it's not one of the famed seven: it is man-made. It consists almost entirely of pieces of big clay jars called amphorae. Millions of them. Probably as many as 25 million.

Anyone used to be able to come up here; now you need a *permesso*. Or the inclination to step over a few chains. From the top we can see the thousand apartment blocks of southern Rome, their rooftops bristling with TV antennas, and dozens of vacant lots, shining with puddles, a Gypsy encampment in one of them, campers and tents, blue tarps snapping against ropes.

Amphorae, when they're found whole, have thin necks, pointed bottoms, two handles. Empty, an unbroken transport amphora weighs sixty-six pounds. In the days of the Empire they'd be filled with wax or honey or linseed or grain, or—more often than not—olive oil. Then they'd be stacked in ships, floated to Rome from Spain or North Africa, dragged up the Tiber, and unloaded right below Mt. Testaccio, before the rapids around Tiber Island. The oil would be decanted into smaller jugs, and the amphorae would be cracked and stuffed with their own pieces and sprinkled with lime and stacked. All regulated, all planned, all recorded in Latin.

Olive oil was the muscle, hair tonic, soap, and lamp fuel of the Empire, the flavor of its meals, the illumination of its dramas. Pliny devotes eight scrupulous chapters of the *Natural History* to olives and the olive tree, from seeding to picking to pressing to storing. Olive oil was rubbed on icons, bridles, kings, pregnant women, and foot sores. Want to preserve a piece of wood? Moisturize your face? Soothe a toothache, alleviate stretch marks, grease a chariot axle, cool your scalp, anoint a dead Christian?

Today Mt. Testaccio is 165 feet high, 236,000 square feet, a monument to appetite as large as any monument in Rome. It's daubed with weeds and a few scrubby trees. The discarded wrappers of candy bars blow past. We roam the summit looking for shards of amphorae, the sun heating the back of our jackets, the wind stripping heat from our hands. The ground chinks beneath our sneakers.

Off to the west, wearing a haze of dark green, is the Janiculum: rooftops and pine trees, a flourish of marble crowned by a tiny iron cross that marks the very top of the Fontanone. To its left is the orange turret that stands on the roof of our apartment building. I think of little Owen and Henry, Owen probably awake from his first nap by now, crawling across the kitchen tiles, tormenting his mother. They haven't been alive a year, and already their diapers are scattered across six states, two continents.

To live is to make leavings. Hair, dust, trash, children, love letters, old shoes, bones. We are all possessed by terrible hungers. When they were less than an hour old, already Henry and Owen knew how to attach themselves to their mother. Rome itself sits on calcareous rocks, the calcite made from the skeletons of trillions of tiny sea animals, their own bodies broken and stacked, literally sprinkled with lime, a primordial cemetery, a pelagic ooze. We are born, we consume, we die. Our landscapes are graveyards, and what is a graveyard if not a landfill?

The weight of the olive oil that arrived in Rome during the six centuries that they stacked amphorae on Mt. Testaccio was something close to 400 million pounds.

Lent: We drink latte *macchiati;* we eat ravioli stuffed with spinach. We soak hunks of a baguette in olive oil we brought back from Umbria, bottled without a label, green and cloudy and sharp.

In restaurants the backs of our chairs scrape the backs of the chairs behind us. On buses we battle for territory with hips and elbows, wedging the stroller through doorways, crushing our calves against wheel wells. A woman weeps in the seat next to me. Shauna overhears someone say, in English, "Well, so what if he's impotent?" A violinist, reeking of wine, drives his instrument case into my back.

Proximity, propinquity—we are not only Americans in Italy, but country people in a big city. I buy a newspaper and turn around and three little girls are stroking the hair of my children. A pair of monks, small as gnomes, push past, talking animatedly, onions on their breath. The piazzas are living rooms and concert halls and festival grounds, the alleys youth lounges, the park benches open-air nurseries. Again and again you are reminded of the architectural necessity for the garden, the cloister, the hidden courtyard.

We run into the man on crutches whose wife is expecting twins. Marco. He is with his daughter. Their doctor, he says, has placed his wife on bed rest. For the past three weeks she has not been allowed to get out of bed except to go to the bathroom.

"And we bought a stroller," he says. "A different one than yours."

His daughter is dark-eyed and curly-haired: beautiful. "Let us know if you need anything," Shauna says, in English.

It's hard to tell if he understands. "Oh, we are doing okay," Marco says. "Aren't we?" and he pats his daughter's shoulder. But his eyes are far away.

On the last day of February, I spend ten entire minutes trying to open a plastic package of Weeble-wobbles Shauna's mother has sent, the boys screaming for me to get them out, my fingers raw, the three little Weebles obstinate in their PVC clamshells. I can't help but wonder, as I saw with a bread knife at the seam of the package, about technology and the sprint that is a modern life. Is progress really a curve that sweeps perpetually higher? Wasn't packaging (or toymaking or cobbling or winemaking or milk or cheese or cement, for that matter) often better three hundred or seven hundred or nineteen hundred years ago?

A few weeks ago, in the Forum, we saw a tour guide stop before an excavation and point with the tip of a folded umbrella. "Notice how the masonry gets better the earlier we go," she said.

Imagine life before industrial milk and government radio and the proliferation of images! Imagine if you only saw the president (or pope or prince or queen) *once* in your life, no television footage, no photographs, just a statue or two, a bust, his profile on a coin. What was life like in Pliny's day? Just think how powerful stories were: Your cousin who saw the emperor galloping toward the Capitoline in his chariot, a pair of fingers held aloft, his face in shadow, guards thundering in his wake, all that bronze flashing in the sunlight. Power, divine right, the radiance of myth—one glimpse in a lifetime, and why wouldn't you believe?

You were born at home. If you were lucky, you died at home. Night beyond the walls was lightless, the sky paralyzed with stars; winter killed family members, and the orb of the planet, a deity in itself, spinning at the center of the universe, glided silently within rings of pestilence and war.

The sound track of life was not the sustained grumble of engines, but the murmur of wind and the howling of dogs, the scolding of mothers; chisels, footfalls, and laughter; the clatter of hooves, the screams of prisoners, and the secrets of neighbors.

Maps were full of shadows. The occasional traveler or soldier might walk away from the neighborhood and return years later with stories either believed or disbelieved or never told, but hardly anyone else ever left. The chimney swift perched on your laundry line would have seen more of your country than you could hope to. Your father's trade would determine practically everything about your life: where you lived, what you did, whom you married, what you ate. Men fought for salt, and the lands to the north, as far as anyone knew, were filled with ice and barbarians. A long walk could take you to the remains of a wall no one would ever cross, because, as Procopius wrote in the sixth century, on the other side "countless snakes and serpents and every other kind of wild creature occupy this area as their own."

The North for the historian Tacitus was nothingness, "a huge and shapeless tract of country." The emperor Caligula's soldiers preferred mutiny to sailing across the English Channel because, they believed, it was so abundantly populated with mermaids. Narwhal tusks were sold as unicorn horns—and why not? It's a lot easier to believe in a horned horse than in a bulbous white whale hunting seals beneath pack ice.

Mastodon bones that turned up in floods were the bones of giants. The phoenix, wrote Pliny, "is as large as an eagle, and has a gleam of gold round its neck and all the rest of it is purple." Lions understood the meaning of prayers, and certain snakes, he claimed, "could catch and gulp down birds passing over them even though they were flying high and fast."

People ate donkey foals, stuffed dormice, stewed larks. There were words you could not say. Witchcraft was real. Asses' milk relieved facial wrinkles; bear fat, mixed with lamp soot, prevented baldness. Scraping your gums with a tooth taken from a man who died a violent death was believed to relieve soreness. Pregnant women who wanted their children to be good-looking were urged to look at good-looking things.

The poet Statius tells this story about the Colosseum: Sometime around AD 81, when the arena was still brand-new, Emperor Domitian threw an all-day drunken bash for the end-of-year festival called Saturnalia. Hazelnuts, dates, plums, and figs rained onto the spectators; servants, white napkins on their arms, distributed free bread and wine. Female gladiators fought, then dwarves; then prostitutes circulated among the stands, and belly dancers, and jugglers. And as the sun was setting, and the general enthusiasm was flagging, the emperor ordered that tens of thousands of exotic birds be released into the stands: flamingos, pheasants, partridges, guinea fowl. The crowd went berserk trying to catch them; there were more birds than spectators, Statius says; it was the ultimate game-day giveaway. Think of it: torchlight flowing under canopies, smoke creeping through archways, feathers flying, birds shrieking, the shouts and scrambling of fifty thousand citizens. And this same Roman sky, framed by the same oval of stone, turning its evening violet, seething with pink flamingos.

I wouldn't trade the twenty-first century for any other. We have toilet paper and pasteurization and Novocain and Mexican avocados all winter long. And plenty of mysteries remain: what causes premature labor, or what exactly the universe is made of. The biology of deep oceans, the nature of gravity, the reason we sleep, the mechanisms of migration; thousands of questions still await answers.

But when I finally get the Weeble-wobbles out of their package, Henry and Owen suck on them for about half a minute, then crawl off, leaving a garishly dressed rhino and alligator wet and rocking on the tile. And I can't help but think of Pliny and modern civilization's persistent assessment of itself as advanced. For if Pliny believed that the moon caused shellfish to wax and wane in size, and women's menses dulled sword blades, and wormwood, worn under a cummerbund, prevented swelling of the groin, so what? Did he not also describe the Earth as a sphere and understand that it rotated every twenty-four hours? Did he not also say, "The only certainty is that nothing is certain?" I'm not reading Pliny to see how far humanity has come as much as I'm reading him to see how much we've lost. Knowledge is relative. Mystery can be cultivated.

Henry and Owen see more images in a day than Pliny saw in a lifetime, and I worry their generation will have to work a bit harder than every previous one to stay alert to the miracles of the world.

Shauna says it's a good thing I didn't get to see snow sifting through the oculus of the Pantheon. Sometimes, she says, the things we don't see are more beautiful than anything else.

It rains, the sun comes out. Five minutes later, hail is bouncing off the street. This morning the Alban Hills were slate blue and velvety. At noon they were shining and white. Now they are heavy and black, terrible, apocalyptic.

Lorenzo crouches in his gatekeeper's lodge, heater blowing, a pile of mail in his lap. "This weather is called monkey weather," he tells us. Shauna and I cross the gravel of the courtyard, on our way to the corner bar to order *spremute,* tall glasses of blood-orange juice. We clasp hands. There is thunder. The west, beyond the Vatican, burns inwardly, a thousand shades of gold.

The oranges are from Sicily. The juice tastes like sunlight: low, red, foamy.

We hold our glasses with two hands. We try not to take anything for granted.

Spring

OWEN AND HENRY SPEND NEARLY ALL THEIR waking minutes preparing to walk. They haul themselves up by drawer handles, inch their palms across cupboard doors. Squat, pivot, tumble: they are gymnasts in training.

On Sundays the big Academy building is quiet and mostly empty, and we lug the boys down the long marble staircase into the basement, which contains offices and a floor of the library and three vaulted brick hallways, each straight as a needle and fifty yards long. I drag an old shopping cart out from beneath one of the stairwells, load Henry in the basket, and position Owen so he can push. Then I let go. Owen walks with his fingers laced through the metal grid, his little moccasins gripping the tile, the cart gliding along. He'll push it down all three hallways, his grin splitting wider and wider, and then Shauna will switch them out and turn the cart around and it will be Henry's turn.

Occasionally, we take breaks for milk.

Before we leave, before we have to strap one child into the backpack and the other into the chest carrier, I'll put them both in the cart and push them as fast as I can, screeching around the corners, hurtling down the straightaways. Our laughter echoes through the vaults, past the stacks of mattresses and broken desks, past the lecture room with its empty chairs, past the antique display cases with Etruscan potsherds scattered inside.

On March 4 the Italian journalist Giuliana Sgrena is released by her kidnappers. The FM stations we usually listen to foam over their normal frequencies, the whole spectrum buzzing, a dozen deejays rattling off faster-than-usual Italian. *Finalmente,* I hear, and *pace,* which means "peace," and the name of the newspaper she writes for, over and over, *Il Manifesto, Il Manifesto.*

Then the news changes. Approaching a checkpoint near the Baghdad airport, Sgrena's Toyota Corolla is fired upon by American soldiers. Sgrena herself is wounded. An Italian security officer, Nicola Calipari, father of two, is killed. "I heard his last breath," Sgrena will write, a few days later, "as he was dying on me."

Who knows what to think? From the terrace every-thing looks the same, the pines tossing in the wind, the *motorini* shooting past. But in the past hour Americans will have become that much less welcome here. Shauna walks Henry out to join me, dangling him by his arms, her hair hanging over his, just the tips of his moccasins touching the ground. "Let's stay in the apartment today," she says.

The next morning our neighbor Jon Piasecki is at the butcher's buying chicken when someone behind him says, *"Sabato con i fascisti."* Saturday with the fascists.

On Tuesday, Calipari's coffin is set on the steps of the Vittoriano. The Italians waiting to see his body fill Piazza

Venezia. CNN.com says thousands have come to pay respects. A Roman paper puts the number at hundreds of thousands. Regardless, from what I can tell, climbing Michelangelo's stairs to the Campidoglio, it's a lot of people. A few rainbow-striped peace flags wave above the crowd; everybody, as all Italians everywhere seem to, wears a navy blue or black coat.

I think of American tourists stuck on buses in the traffic this must be causing and wonder about the strange intersections of nations. One of the Iraqi kidnappers, Sgrena says, was a fan of Rome's soccer club. The airport road the Italians were driving is referred to in the papers as Route Irish. One of the American soldiers at the checkpoint, the one operating the gun in what was called the "blocking vehicle," is a father of two named Mario Lozano. *Mario* comes from *Marius,* a Roman name, centuries old.

Spring here comes fast, a barbarian invasion, a Japanese harbor wave. I blink and the grass has turned green. We're walking home from a restaurant, passing alongside the Fontanone, when I realize the chimney swifts are back.

My overcrowded tulip bulbs awaken in their pots, one after another, showing pale green shoots. Ivy laces old walls; the trees in the gardens are locked in an invisible frenzy: light rains on the branches, moisture hurls upward through trunks, roots suck at stones. Color flies into the eye: sepia walls, red roof-tiles, emerald lawns—it is as if, all along, an illumination box has been mounted above the city and finally somebody has plunked a coin into the slot.

Two weeks before Easter I fly to London to appear on a television show. I have a note in my pocket that says

Good luck, Daddy in Shauna's handwriting and has scribbling all over it. When I return, forty hours later, pale brown mushrooms have appeared overnight in the hydrangea bed beside our building's entrance. My tulips are suddenly four inches tall. I look up from feeding Owen breakfast to find a pair of ladybugs mating on my sleeve.

Days of rain. I wake at 2 a.m. and type the ending to the story I've been working on, writing through the night, backtracking around dead-ends, linking together fragmented sections.

In the morning, down in Trastevere, the river slips its banks, rushing brown and foaming over the jogging paths beneath the embankments. Cormorants dive one by one into the rapids around Tiber Island and emerge with little brown eels squirming in their beaks.

Indeed, the whole city seems to be filling up, breath after breath of springtime blowing off the hills, piles of artichokes appearing at the vegetable stand, then fava beans, then strawberries, as if a sequence of northbound waves is breaking over the city. The austerity of Lent gives way: Romans pour out of their houses and swirl through the streets, throng the markets in Testaccio, sit hip to hip along the benches outside the Palazzo Farnese, devouring gelati. And the tourists return, too, trampling through the Pantheon, circling the Forum. One afternoon the parking garage at the Vatican bus stop is virtually empty; the next it is stuffed with buses.

In the second week of March I walk to the bakery practicing vocabulary. *Glassa* is icing; *compleanno* is birthday. I insert one edge of myself into the queue and slip, like a needle, to the front. One *torta,* please. *Cioccolata.* With icing. For thirty people.

Shauna hauls a handcart full of beer and wine the half mile home from the grocery store. I spend two nights drawing invitations. We buy Mylar balloons. We buy a Chicco Play 'N Ride Car Deluxe with rocker and safety bar and carry it up from Trastevere from the toy store, and Shauna wraps it in shining Italian wrapping paper.

Owen stands in the playpen and bounces while we chant "Jump, jump, jump!" Henry cries in his crib, in his high chair. He runs the tip of his tongue from one side of his mouth to the other and back again; he grinds his finger against the swollen rims of his gums.

Then it's March 18 and the boys are one year old. The cake, when I pick it up, is the size of a small desk. I carry it up via Carini, through the whizzing traffic, and into the park across the street from our apartment. We set up high chairs and tables; we tie balloons to the gate. The trees send hazy shadows across the lawn.

Friends come, mostly Americans. Lorenzo the gate-keeper wanders out of the *portineria,* wearing beautiful tan shoes and jeans and his big, eye-warping glasses. Tacy rides the bus an hour each way to bring the boys a yellow plastic shoe that plays music. It will become their favorite toy.

We sing "Happy Birthday" in English, then Italian. Owen grins at me from across the park, cake all down his front, his hair flattened across his ears. Henry spends a half hour crying, overwhelmed, in one of the swings. Soon enough everyone is gone and we are folding paper cups into trash bags. On the terrace I spray the high chairs with a hose. Twelve months ago tonight, Shauna held Owen in a hospital bed, snow flying past the window. I sat beside Henry in the NICU down the hall, a hospital gown over my T-shirt, a dozen monitors beeping around us, my fingers on the Plexiglas. The circumference of his wrist was smaller than the circumference of my pinkie finger. Now he pushes the horn on his new plastic car and his brother sings his vowels as he crawls, squealing, toward the bathtub.

After they're in their cribs, after all the dishes are done, we open a bottle of Prosecco and pour it into two water glasses. It is the color of straw. Tiny bubbles fly upward. I spend a couple minutes with a calculator. In the past year Shauna breast-fed for approximately 1,040 hours. She put the boys down for 1,460 naps. She did something close to four tons of laundry. I folded maybe four pounds of that.

It's Henry and Owen's birthday, but the toast is for their mother.

Two days after Henry and Owen turn one, the war in Iraq turns two. We are walking from the Pantheon toward Piazza Colonna when we catch the tail end of a peace march. Maybe three hundred carabinieri in riot gear mill between trucks; one passes what look like machine guns up through an open door. A helicopter floats above. Protesters, at the far end of the street, hold painted bedsheets and sing. I imagine I can feel their eyes on us, on the stroller. We are Americans, I want to say, but America is a big place.

The next day is Palm Sunday. The newspapers doubt

the pope will be well enough to make an appearance, but he manages to sit for a minute in his apartment window, a few stories above St. Peter's Square. His face is the same color as his white alb; he seems to be pressing the heel of his hand into his forehead. Boys wave flags and chant, *"Viva la Papa!"* Long live the pope. Some even surf atop the outstretched arms of their friends.

He does not speak. Still, the crowd roars. After he recedes, something like exaltation radiates from the faces around me. Celebrity, the cult of recognition. Denzel Washington getting miked up on Thirty-seventh Street, women screaming his name.

Whenever the stroller passes a cat, Owen grins his two-and-a-half-toothed grin and shouts, "Deedeedee!" (his version of "kitty"). Whenever we open the terrace door, Henry screams in delight. They sit in their high chairs, wind pouring through the windows, and pinch pieces of tortellini between their thumbs and forefingers and fumble them into their fists and drop them on the floor.

We eat *broccolo Romano,* a pale, diminutive broccoli. We try *puntarelle,* thin, sweet chicory shoots soaked in oil and vinegar. Everything surges. The lawns are a supernatural green. It is as if I can hear roots crackling and rustling in the flower beds.

In high spring, my tree guidebook says, inside a mature oak tree, rising sap can reach velocities of two hundred feet per hour. That's three feet a minute. I lean over the windowsill of the studio and stare at the big trunk of the Italian pine and wonder about its thirst, its cloud of half a billion root tips prowling through the soil.

At dusk a pair of hawk moths like little winged lobsters hover in the Academy courtyard, sucking nectar from the jasmine. At night Trastevere distends with young people, a drummer pounding bongos with demonic stamina, children sprinting through the mobs. Every bakery and *fruttivendolo,* every supermarket and husband-and-wife *salumeria,* hangs enormous foil-wrapped chocolate eggs from the ceiling. Vermilion eggs, silver eggs, Donald Duck eggs with the diameter of a dinner plate. *Gran Sorpresa!* they say, Big Surprise! Trapped inside are toys: rocket-men and soccer players, little incarcerated acrylic pandas.

The birds, singing on the gutters in the morning, are loud enough to wake us. In his crib, Henry pulls himself up by the slats and lets his right hand dangle at his side, bouncing on his mattress, testing, practicing.

On Easter Sunday we melt the shell of an infant-sized chocolate egg and dip strawberries in it and set them on foil to dry. Only in Italy would the chocolate from an egg containing two red plastic robots taste good enough to make you want to cry. Shauna dips a finger in the warm chocolate and slips it into Henry's mouth, and his face seems to crack open with wonder. He looks at his mother as if to say, You've been putting green beans on my tray and the world includes *this*?

All across the country, birds are making nests, rising up corridors of nectar, chasing the northward tide of blooms. Love, something sweet to eat, and the quickening of the heart. What else is springtime about?

In the afternoon a man clambers over the tourist railing on the cupola at the very top of St. Peter's Basilica, several hundred feet above the roof of the church below, and crouches on the impossibly steep face of the dome. Fire-fighters close the church; a bishop tries to talk him down.

Helicopters buzz past the terrace. The air glitters with pollen.

Before nightfall we stroll the boys through Villa Sciarra, the fountains splashing, the hedges wearing a haze of light, the cypresses casting stately shadows. Families promenade all around us, wearing Easter finery, laughing, gesturing, eating ice-cream bars. On the way home we pass two teenagers making out in a Volkswagen. Two cars down, another couple is lying on top of one another, four legs in jeans and sneakers sticking out a window.

"Italians," our friend George Stoll says, "will stop anything for pleasure." And the longer we're here, the more we feel he's right. Espresso, silk pajamas, a five-minute kiss; the sleekest, thinnest cell phone; extremely smooth leather. Truffles. Yachts. Four-hour dinners.

The following recipe for a Nutella Dog, submitted by twelve-year-old Martina Bartolozzi, appeared in the newspaper the other day. Nutella is a hazelnut-flavored chocolate spread that Italians spread on everything: toast, crepes, breadsticks, cookies, even pizza *bianca*.

1. Spread the cut sides of a hot dog bun with Nutella.
2. Fill bun with peeled banana "dog."
3. Enjoy.

The third step is the important one, the *piacere,* the "enjoy."

Shauna and I bring the stroller up via Carini in the last

light of the day and reach the Porta San Pancrazio. We are crossing the street when our tires grind over powdered glass in the dimples of the asphalt. I crouch for a second; the glass is nearly gone, hardly more than sand. The awful smacking sound comes back to me, the sirens, the little rental Peugeot smashed against the travertine.

"Only he who always remembers how frail a thing man is will weigh life in an impartial balance," Pliny said. In his day, life was terribly fragile: infant mortality, scholars have estimated, was 300 in 1,000: that is, about 30 percent of all live-born babies died within the first year. A mean life-expectancy was only twenty-five. Death was everywhere. It's no wonder Pliny devotes so many pages to honey, the different varieties, the best times to collect it, its sweetness so intoxicating because it was so fleeting, and even now, nearly twenty centuries later, Romans seem far more aware of their own evanescence than Americans do. Romans discuss death over dinner; they wait in line to examine the corpses of their dead heroes; they take the arms of revered old parents and escort them through the parks on Sundays. Six or seven times, since coming to Italy, I've seen young people on park benches reading novels to grandmothers. I've seen hundred-year-old women picking stolidly through eggplants at the market, or dragging pull-along grocery carts up hills on ruined ankles, or slumped in piazzas under shawls with whirlpools of suffering turning in their eyes.

Decay of republic, disintegration of empire, the ongoing crumble of Church—death is the river that runs through town, driving along beneath the bridges, roiling in the rapids beside the hospitals on Tiber Island. Death is in the stains on the walls; it's the weight of Keats's tombstone upon the sod, the permission slip Romans sign when a long-haired girl climbs onto the back of her boyfriend's Vespa, when the banker puts the transmission in park and takes the librarian in his arms. I agree to live now, live as sweetly as I can, to fill my clothes with wind and my eyes with lights, but I understand I'll have to leave in the end.

We Americans, with our closed-door executions and gated retirement communities, are the ones who seem to have a hard time thinking about death. I picture the man crouched atop St. Peter's a half mile away, 435 feet of open air beneath his shoelaces, who knows what fatigue in his heart, gravity tugging at him, Easter Sunday slipping away, two or three helicopters ratcheting over his head. The view beyond the tips of his eyelashes is on postcards all over the world: the arms of Bernini's colonnade, Mussolini's via della Conciliazione, the bisecting thread of the river, and the apartments of Rome fading off into darkness.

If he slips, if he pushes off, what will he think as the roof of the church hurtles toward his face?

Finally?

If only I'd had time, had children, had better shoes?

Or, Thank you, thank you, thank you?

He doesn't jump. The firefighters lasso him and haul him back over the railing. He is forty-five years old and still lives with his mother. She is in the papers most of the week, thanking God.

But death is still in the air. Five days after Easter the pope's condition has deteriorated significantly. In a city of nuns, I've never seen so many: nuns in khaki, nuns in blue, nuns in crisp, dazzling white. In front of St. Peter's, they stand in groups of three or four, talking quietly. I pass one, pulling a rosary through her fingers, with the most intense black eyes I have ever seen, gazing up at the windows of the pope's apartments. It is as if her eyes are going to burn right out of her face and go rising up into the sunlight.

There are maybe a thousand people, all told, inside the colonnade. Hardly anyone is sitting. Most of them face the windows of the papal apartments. Everything is quiet—quiet enough to hear the water pouring into the basins of the fountains. A flag flaps lightly, and pigeons rise past the obelisk.

A street away, in front of Castle Sant'Angelo, at least a hundred white vans are parked bumper to bumper, each with a satellite dish on the roof. Cameramen in vests chew *panini;* two reporters share a hot dog.

Today seems an especially bad day to die: the first of April, and the weather is perfect, the apples and nectarines flowering, the persimmons just starting. Spring is not so much a season in Rome as an onslaught of colors: silver, gold, green.

I look up at John Paul's bedroom and think, If his bed is near the window, he can watch clouds soaring past the cupola—huge anvils of cumulus, pale and full of shoulders. The wind slowly tears them to shreds. Thin blades of light slip through and touch down everywhere.

The following day is Saturday. The front three pages of every newspaper are about the pope. The *Corriere della Sera* runs twenty-six pages of coverage. Even on the pop stations they talk about him, machine-gun bursts of Italian between Lionel Richie and the Bee Gees. *Il Papa,* they say, *il Papa.* In his apartment he's burning up, lungs failing, kidneys failing. Every person we run into seems to know something new. He's conscious, he's unconscious, he's recognizing his staff, he's not in a coma. Already they've given him the Sacrament of the Infirm, and the special Communion you only get when you're hours away.

It seems impossible but today is more beautiful than yesterday. The sky is a depthless, flawless cobalt. Everywhere little chamomile daisies open their white faces to the sun—the lawns look as if they're covered with snow.

A breeze lifts great clouds of pollen out of the cypresses. Bells toll. Around the world, prayers gather and fly toward us, hurrying past our windows on the way to the Vatican from Brazil, from China, from Poland.

More than three miles of artwork hang in the Vatican Museums, and the pope could have any of it brought in front of him: a Raphael, a Michelangelo, a Caravaggio, a Fra Angelico. Instead he wants only to hear something read from the Bible in Polish.

By noon, maybe fifty thousand people are gathered in the piazza, gazing up at the windows of his apartment.

After dinner, after the boys are asleep, I walk down to the Vatican one more time. It is the hour of the *passeggiata* and the streets are crowded. Most everyone is beautifully dressed: glossy shoes, sport jackets, long skirts. Down the entire quarter mile of via della Conciliazione, camera lights glow white. Maybe a thousand lenses are aimed toward the basilica. Women with designer handbags give interviews; priests in white give interviews. Pigeons wheel above the fountains. Everyone seems to be waiting, and every journalist seems to be trying to make a story out of the waiting.

The sky is that heartbreaking violet you see only on very clear nights, violet pocked with a few warm stars. Figures mill on rooftops, on top of the colonnade. Candles burn here and there.

More people are crammed into the square than on Christmas Day or Easter—I'd guess sixty thousand. Three windows of the pope's apartments are lit. Along the whole top floor, only those windows glow. I can't help but wonder if things are frantic behind his curtains, if doctors are rushing back and forth.

Maybe a dozen priests gather on the left side of the basilica steps and take turns praying quietly into a microphone. Mostly they do Rosaries, Hail Marys, over and over. The crowd murmurs along.

Men with fifty-pound cameras push past us. They say John Paul II was the first pope to live in the twenty-four-hour media cycle, and it's obvious he's dying in one. Everything is filmed; everyone is filming. Raised arms hold cell phones, digital cameras. If the pope could look over his sill, he'd see a sea of faces strobed by a thousand flashbulbs, his ashen face transformed into pixels and channeled through lenses into cables and air, into the instant-transmission scrutiny of the world.

This is the pope who reputedly joked, "If it didn't happen on television, it didn't happen." Well, this is happening. Four oversize screens mounted in the piazza show pilgrims, show the cathedral, show a close-up of St. Peter's stone beard. A bald man in Nikes and a suit stands a little apart, his head bowed. As I watch, two separate photographers crouch in front of him and take a dozen exposures each.

In front of the basilica, one of the priests, a young man, takes the microphone and sings a song I don't recognize. His voice is almost impossibly sweet. The crowd sings along. I shut my eyes. There is something very real about this moment, despite the cameras, despite the spectacle— something of the stillness that exists beneath the helter-skelter commotion of Rome, and I don't mean only in the catacombs or the deep corners of cathedrals, or out in the countryside along fallen arcades of aqueducts, but that rises now and then from a piazza in the middle of a winter day, or from an umbrella pine early in the morning— a hush that creeps out of the earth and fills your heart with something like peace.

The pope dies just after nine thirty that evening, April 2. Inside his apartment, a cardinal says his name three times. A startlingly beautiful girl in denim beside me weeps silently. Bells begin to clang, or maybe it's just one bell, up on the left side of the basilica, swaying heavily back and forth. It echoes off the cobbles, off the pillars, off the gathered heads.

I think maybe I'll see something thin and glorious slip out of the sky, but nothing comes. The piazza is quiet, except for the bell and the water spilling into the fountains. I think of Henry and Owen, a mile away, asleep behind their doors. I think, This is going to happen to all of us.

People pour into Rome. Within a day the streets around the Vatican are mobbed. The radio guesses 2 million pilgrims are coming; the Internet guesses 3. All along the Janiculum, apartments are rented out. Hotels are overbooked. We hear that Katie Couric is staying down the street; we see Americans in vests at the Bar Gianicolo, a little café beside the Porta San Pancrazio, ordering Pepsis.

Despite the furor, I work nonstop on my short story, crashing through a fifth draft, then a sixth, oscillating between exhilaration and despair.

One minute I think, This here, this is a good sentence. The next I am on the brink of throwing the whole thing away. But I am used to this by now.

Three nights after the death of the pope, Shauna and I watch a DVD on our computer. The boys are asleep. The city is stuffed with visitors; impromptu campgrounds are springing up in fairgrounds, a concert hall, an empty railway building. We are near the end of the movie when Shauna says, "I don't feel well."

"What do you mean?"

"My neck is tingling. Everything is tingling."

She blinks and starts fanning her face. Her fingers, I notice, are very pale. She climbs out of bed. She gets back in. I glance at the clock: 10:31 p.m. I stop the movie.

"I don't feel well," she says again, and splotches of pink bloom and fade on her throat. I run to get her a glass of water, and by the time I bring it to her she has climbed out of bed again. She hurries across the room. She sets the glass on the kitchen table. She tries to shake feeling into her fingers. Then her eyes go blank and she falls over.

One moment, but a moment in which you can feel the globe stop and pivot, and that enormous eye of God stare through the atmosphere and clouds and roof and ceiling, through your clothes and skin, and fix on the blind, self-deluded creature in the dark that is you.

Our little kitchen seems frozen in a terrible, silvered light. Shauna is lying on the baby blankets in front of the couch, one knee caught beneath her. Miraculously, her head has come to rest on a folded corner of blanket. I wonder about the pope and three days and reincarnation. Waves of panic build along the horizon.

I drag Shauna onto the couch. She is conscious again maybe five seconds later, but her eyes are strange. Silky. She has begun to shiver badly—not like a seizure, but with that kind of intensity. I pin her fingers between mine. Her palms are cold.

"You fainted," I say. I am trying to believe it.

She whispers, "I can't breathe." But she is breathing. I pile blankets on top of her. I cram thick socks onto her feet. Twelve feet away Owen sleeps in his bathroom, and Henry sleeps in the room next to that.

Doctors, I think, doctors. I know a few from college. A friend's father in Boise is a neurologist. Is it morning there? I fumble through pages in my address book. The sequence of numbers I need to dial to reach the United States has fled my brain. 0–001? 0–11? Shauna trembles beneath her blankets—three of them, all the blankets we have. Wouldn't it be easier to pretend this had never happened? Wouldn't it be easier if we were home and I could put her in our own car and drive her five minutes to the emergency room?

"Do you need to go to the hospital, Shauna? Do you think you need to go to the hospital?"

Her teeth jackhammer against each other. "I'm scared," she says.

I don't remember everything that happens next. I call the gatekeeper, Norm, who calls a taxi. I call Laura, our lovely, fearless neighbor, who is in our hallway in a minute. I am explaining about the boys' milk, the boys' bottles, but she is already waving me out the door.

Somehow we get to the sidewalk. Somehow another Academy fellow, Sean, and an Italian man I have not met have heard we need help. They sit with us on the Academy steps. The nearest emergency room is Regina Margherita, on viale Trastevere, less than a mile away. Shauna has our yellow fleece blanket around her shoulders. In the quiet I can hear her teeth clacking.

The taxi driver drives like every Italian taxi driver and we are inside the hospital in perhaps two minutes. They admit her with a wave of the hand. A short, calm nurse in sneakers ushers us into an examination room. He retrieves a doctor. The doctor is tall and sleepy-looking. He smells of mothballs. My sledgehammer Italian fails us: I cannot describe tingling, or losing consciousness, or the inability to breathe. The word I know for "faint" is *indistinto*.

I try, *"La mia moglie, lei è indistinta."* My wife, she is indistinct. Eventually Sean's Italian friend comes in from the waiting room and rescues us.

The doctor examines. Our new friend translates. I pray. I love my wife but I am ashamed to admit that the prayers I send up are selfish. What if I have to take care of our babies alone? Every minute tied to them, no one to spell me, no one to laugh with, no one to ask, when they wake crying at 4 a.m., "Do we just let them cry?" No one to keep the other baby happy as I change a diaper on the cobbles of Piazza Navona?

Widower with Twins: a lousy, short-lived sitcom.

The doctor asks Shauna to hold out her tongue. He puts drops on it to make her *tranquillo*. I ask if she can have another blanket. After a half hour or so, she has finally stopped shivering. The little nurse spends a long time probing Shauna's forearm with a needle, trying to find a vein, and my wife lies mildly sedated on a table in her thick socks, and our Italian friend goes green and has to sit down in another room, and I pace and wonder about my sons sleeping up on the hill and about the little scraps of trash—wadded tissues, the backings of Band-Aids— gathered in the corners of the examination room. I try to get Shauna to rehash her day, when she ate, when she drank water, but she is drugged now and scared and a five-foot-tall man in Reeboks is repeatedly jabbing her forearm with a needle.

Eventually we realize she had only one glass of water all day. Nothing to drink since lunch.

"We have two babies," I tell the doctor. "Twins." He looks at Shauna and cocks his head, as if computing this. Or perhaps my Italian is so bad I have told him something else. This is a persistent fear in Italy, that I am insulting people, that I am giving incorrect directions, asking for more grapefruit sauce.

I tell the nurse a joke, in English: "What do you call someone who speaks two languages? Bilingual. What do you call someone who speaks one language? American."

He doesn't laugh. They finally draw blood. They give her an IV. They give her an EKG. They ask me questions about menstruation I don't understand and I think they are wondering if she is pregnant. The doctor says he'd like to keep her *tutta la notte*. All the night.

At one in the morning in a foreign hospital the mind wanders down thorny paths. Brain tumor? Neurological disorder? Auspices, omens: the great, all-knowing eye peers into us from miles away and knows everything there is to know.

"Maybe you're just worn out from the boys," I tell Shauna.

"Maybe," she says.

We hold hands. Her bed is wheeled into an elevator that smells of urine. The elevator rasps upward and she is taken down a hall and through a doorway. An orderly flips on lights. Two women, in two other beds, groan awake and twist in their sheets.

The orderly positions Shauna's bed in the corner, tells us something I don't understand, then flips the lights back off and leaves. The women sniffle. The one by the window is big and, I think, quite old. She begins to cough. The window looks down onto viale Trastevere, at almost exactly the place we saw the man and the Newfoundland get on the *motorino*. There is traffic even now: cars, a bus, a half-empty tram shuttling past, a girl standing in the last car, her palms pressed to the window.

The room has only the three beds and two IV stands and a radiator with its paint peeling off in long, deciduous strips. No chairs. The bathroom is down the hall. Shauna is pale, pale; she looks as if she were deposited into the bottom right of Michelangelo's *Last Judgment,* forms and faces tumbling through the blue, cowering before the ferryman's horrible paddle. "Whereas the signs of death are innumerable," Pliny wrote in a chapter on disease, "there are no signs of health being secure."

The old woman rattles off chains of coughs. The other is quiet. Shauna's IV drips silently, the bag imperceptibly deflating. A moan echoes down the hall. I alternate squatting on the floor and sitting on the edge of the bed. I feel paranoid and raw, twelve months of sleeplessness chewing away at me. Laura is watching the boys and they're probably asleep anyway, but I'm deeply uncomfortable being away from them; I feel as though they are suddenly vulnerable. As if we have been skating all this time in Italy across a barely frozen pond, and now the ice has finally given way.

Neither of the nurses I can find speak English. I ask for water and am given an empty cup. I steal a blanket from an empty bed in another room and put it over Shauna's feet. I pour tap water into her mouth.

Shauna has been in her room a half hour when a nurse enters, flips on the lights, and—I am pretty sure—tells me I cannot stay the night. There is more groaning from the other beds. I pretend I don't understand. The nurse puts her hands on her hips, looks at a clipboard, and flips off the light. I can hear her move down the ward, the soles of her shoes squeaking.

Breathing. Traffic. The groaning of the elevator. "I'm scared," Shauna whispers. Her eyes reflect a streetlight.

"I know."

"What's wrong with me?"

"Nothing's wrong with you. You need to rest. They're putting fluids back into you."

"But the boys."

"The boys are fine."

The old woman coughs and coughs. I begin to get the feeling the coughing is aimed at us, at our lack of consideration. It is around two when I leave and the IV bag is empty and Shauna is miles from sleep. I hurry up the empty staircases, beneath the dark trees, running the last quarter mile past the Fontanone, its blue water churning on and on.

Owen is up at five forty-five. By five fifty he has already had a bowel movement and dragged a cup full of water off the kitchen table and drenched his pajamas.

I telephone Tacy, who is able to come by ten thirty. Laura is sleepy, but able to take the boys at seven. When I leave, they are in their high chairs throwing Honey Nut Cheerios onto the floor and laughing. I jog to the hospital, through the entrance, up the stairs, and into Shauna's room, signing nothing, seeing nobody. Shauna looks infinitely better. They have put a second bag of fluids into her during the night, and the pink in her cheeks is back. The old woman is still coughing; the younger woman is sitting up, talking into a cell phone. By nine no one has come to speak with us. We wait and wait. To enter a hospital in Italy, we learn, is to relinquish all sovereignty over time.

"Do you feel okay?"

"I feel better. I feel fine."

"Are you pregnant?"

"No." She looks at me. "I don't think so."

"Do you feel well enough to leave?"

"Probably. But don't we want to know what happened?"

We wait another half hour. We are fine. Everything is going to be fine. I buy croissants and orange juice. Pina, the Academy's assistant director of operations, a warm, animated woman who loves our boys, comes to sit with us around eleven.

Farther down the ward, in a room identical to Shauna's, I see a trio of doctors moving between beds. One scribbles on a clipboard, one asks questions, one takes a pulse. But another half hour passes and no one comes into our room.

The city, Pina tells us, is glutted with pilgrims. The wait to get into the basilica to view the pope's body is almost twenty-four hours. The city estimates that nearly 2 million mourners have come from Poland alone. Pina waited in line for eight hours yesterday and did not even reach the piazza. Police have started turning back pilgrims who try to get in the back of the line, she says. His body will be buried before they can reach it. Authorities are text-messaging every cell subscriber in Rome: Stay away.

Get in line on Wednesday; still in line on Friday.

Around two, the trio of doctors finally enters our room. They spend a long time with the coughing woman in the corner, asking her questions, listening to her chest. Nothing is rushed—there are no *stats,* no blood-spattered nurses sprinting in with bad news. Eventually they come over to us, listen to Pina awhile, then ask Shauna questions. Pina laughs, the doctors laugh. Shauna and I follow very little, nodding with half-open mouths, waiting for Pina to turn to us. It is an awful feeling, actually, to cling to what you suspect must be a pronouncement of your fate, your wife's fate, and yet not be entirely sure the discussion isn't about a television program. I study Pina's face, her busy mouth, her big eyes. I hear the female doctor say *soleggiato,* "sunny." Sunny? Is this the diagnosis?

"Pina," I say. "We aren't following."

She pats Shauna's hand. "They say they are fairly confident that dehydration and exhaustion brought on the fainting spell," she says. "And that you subsequently had an anxiety attack."

We exhale. Dehydration. Exhaustion. She is not pregnant. Essentially the diagnosis is one we already know: twins. Shauna is discharged an hour later. Before we leave, I fill out one form, the size of an index card, writing down our address, the number on my permit of stay, and our passport numbers. We will never receive a bill.

At home, I pay Tacy, who seems entirely unperturbed by the event, as if Filipina mothers are always fainting, no big deal. Every time I am around Tacy, I am reminded of the stories about Raphael, who apparently was perpetually calm, never angry with his assistants; he was handsome and understated and wrote sweet letters to importunate dukes explaining why a painting or tapestry would be late. And yet he died of overwork at age thirty-seven.

Shauna takes a shower, plays with Henry and Owen awhile, then climbs into bed.

The twins crawl to me, rest their heads in my lap. Their soft flesh; their sticky fingers. I read them *Big Fish, Little Fish;* I try to imagine myself as a single parent. I push the stroller to the wine shop on Carini, buy two cases of water, load the big bottles into the baskets beneath the stroller, and push it sweating back through the streets. I stop in the garden behind the Academy and let the boys crawl through the grass.

The heads of the pines loom over us, complicated and gauzy. I remember, precisely and for the first time, what a friend, standing in our kitchen back in Boise, said to Shauna the day before we left: "Not many people would just up and move to Italy with two babies, you know."

Back then I thought it was just a thing to say.

At dusk, bats pour out of archways and swoop past the terrace, flying in shadowy arcs. Night seeps through the trees, the windows, the mind.

I think I know some Italian and then my wife collapses in the kitchen and I realize I know nothing. I can say "This stroller is made in New Zealand" and "I would like to reserve a table for two," but I can't ask "Why was she shivering so violently?" or "What, fundamentally, is the status of my wife's health?" because I can't formulate the questions and won't comprehend the answers. So I stay inside the walls of *Sì* and *No* and *Buongiorno* and *Buona sera,* confined to my own crimped versions of the city, trying to learn what I can by peering through a keyhole now and then. There is the woman and her husband who feed the stray cats in front of our building every night, pulling up in their white van and whistling softly and setting out foil packets of boiled meat. There is the kind face of the butcher in his Tecnica ski hat, and his bleached-blond and machine-tanned son, whom we call Jude Law, wearing his surfing necklace, peering into his ringing cell phone and rolling his eyes at me and shouting, in English, "Girlfriend again!" There's Maria at the pasta shop, and our friend Lavinia at the Academy's photo archive, and Marco the expectant father of twins, and good old Lorenzo the gatekeeper. But do I really *know* any of them? Can I say that I understand any of their lives?

We came to Rome because we'd always regret it if we didn't, because every timidity eventually turns into regret. But the enormity of what I don't know about this place never ceases to amaze me. In 1282, the Tuscan monk Ristoro d'Arezzo declared, "It is a dreadful thing for the inhabitants of a house not to know how it is made." Dreadful, indeed. What I think he meant was that we ought to understand the earth we live on, its skies, its stones. We ought to understand why we live the lives we live. But I don't even understand the apartment building in which I live. How is linoleum made? Or window glass, or porcelain? By what power does water rise to the third floor and pour out of this faucet?

Forget the house, how about the body? Arteriosclerosis, embolism, thrombosis, infarction—I don't know what any of those things are. Do we really know that Shauna fainted because she was tired? Or did she faint because a little clot is wandering the tunnels of her arteries, waiting to stop up her blood supply and finish her off?

And what about Rome? Rome is beautiful, Rome is ugly. Something about this city exacerbates contrasts, the incongruities and contradictions, a Levi's billboard rippling on the façade of a four-hundred-year-old church, a drunk sleeping on the tram in $300 shoes. Four mornings ago I watched a man chat with the baker for five minutes while a half dozen of us waited behind him, then climb into a Mercedes and tear off at fifty miles an hour. As if he had not a single second to spare.

Ciao, ciao. Buongiorno, buongiorno. I understand less about Italy now than I did in November. Maybe I understand less about Italy now than I did when I was seven, filling in the outlines of the Colosseum in a coloring book.

What is Rome? It's a place where a grown man can drive a tiny car called a Panda or Musa (the Muse) or Punto (the Dot) or Stilo (the Stylus) or Picasso.

It's a feast every damned week. It's maddening retail hours. It's a city about to become half old-people's home/half tourist museum. It's like America before coffee was "to go," when a playground was a patch of gravel, some cigarette butts, and an uninspected swing set; when everybody smoked; when businesses in your neighborhood were owned by people who lived in your neighborhood; when children still stood on the front seats of moving cars and spread their fingers across the dash. It's a public health-care service that ensures assistance to both Italians and foreigners in an equal manner and allows a doctor to make a decision such as keeping Shauna overnight without having to worry about costing her several thousand dollars. It's our friend Cristiano Urbani, who is the first male in his family in at least four generations not to become a fishmonger. "You know," he says, "they get up so early in the morning. And they always smell like fish!" It's an economy in recession, the lowest birthrate in Europe (1.3 children per woman), 40 percent of thirty- to thirty-four-year-olds still living with their parents. It's a place where stoplights are open to interpretation, lattes should never be ordered after lunch, and a man is not considered a failure if he's forty years old and still spinning dough in a pizzeria. It's a country where parents let their kids play soccer in the streets and walk home from school unaccompanied, where your first thought when you see an adult man talking to a child in the street is not necessarily *Child molester.*

One block I feel as though I'm unraveling the hyphae of some elemental memory, ivy swinging from Michelangelo's unfinished bridge behind the Palazzo Farnese, water pouring from a satyr's mouth into an upturned scallop shell—meaning is reverberating through the stones, a key is slipping into a keyhole, and the largest gate between me and this city is finally going to open.

The next block I see two men in zippered leather with rings through their lips dropping rocks off the Ponte Sisto at passing joggers, and I think, There is nothing here I'll ever understand.

Che carini. Che belli. The moon gleams above the terrace. Right now, from every direction, from Europe, from South America, from Africa, people stream into Rome to mourn one dead man, to glimpse an incandescent, two-thousand-year-old mystery. And I walk around as though kidnapped by insurgents, beauty streaming through the edges of the blindfold. As I watch, one after another, five, then six, then seven swifts dive into the throat of a chimney.

"Though you are a whole world, Rome," Goethe wrote in 1790, "still, without love, the world's not the world, Rome cannot be Rome."

A spring night is a power that sweeps through the crowded sheaves of blooming tulips and pours into your heart like a river.

On the morning of the pope's funeral, April 8, three fighter jets roar over the apartment, rattling dishes in the cupboards. Helicopters float above the Vatican.

Shauna looks better, makes jokes, lugs both boys around in her arms. I work all morning on a book review, then walk the crest of the Janiculum, past the big statue of Garibaldi on horseback, past the pedestals and busts of all his lieutenants, down the steep, narrow alley plunging toward the Tiber. Still I don't see the throngs, not the way the news keeps telling us to expect: between 4 and 5 million mourners, a four-kilometer queue to see John Paul's body, twenty mourners—exhausted, dehydrated—fainting every hour.

Then I reach the river. Volunteers in fluorescent green, many wearing fedoras with feathers stuck in the bands, block the street. There is no entering any of the streets I might ordinarily use to approach the basilica. Ambulances and military vehicles idle in intersections; everything is sealed off. To get any closer I'll have to cross the Tiber and work my way around to the Vatican from the far bank.

Along the bridge closest to me, the Ponte Principe Amedeo Savoia Aosta, candles stand along the length of the parapets, dead inside red glass. Pilgrims drowse on the cobbles: a group of college kids, women in beach chairs, a collared priest wearing what looks like snowpants. The water below is pale green, wrinkled silver with sunlight. A plywood plank the width and length of a minivan travels slowly downstream.

The riverside plane trees on the far side are dropping so many seeds, the air seems filled with snow. The seeds tap softly against the lenses of my sunglasses. A fireboat trolls by, then a police boat. Dust blows up from the media depot by Castle Sant'Angelo.

People walk about with sleeping bags folded in their

arms. Tents line the jogging path. Every tenth pilgrim I pass is carrying a big overnight backpack or dragging a suitcase on wheels. Nearly everyone has the glassy, hollow look you get when you've slept on something too hard and awakened too early for too many days in a row.

The Ponte Vittorio Emanuele II is completely cordoned off. On the next bridge upriver, the Ponte Sant'Angelo, pilgrims are packed shoulder to shoulder. I squeeze in. Dozens of radios play, all tuned to the same station. Everyone is slow and calm, facing the same direction. An altar boy with a sign in Polish squeezes past. Two nuns sit hugging their knees on a sheet of cardboard. Someone beside the pope's body, a half mile away, finishes a speech, and applause reverberates through the radios and hisses out of distant speakers, erected on scaffolding.

It takes me fifteen minutes to get across the bridge. On the other side, along the fringes of the crowd, men sell whatever they can: John Paul dinner plates, John Paul T-shirts, John Paul heads molded from plastic, a misaligned seam bisecting his face. Thousands and thousands of people clutch newsprint copies of the pope's will in different languages—as if he were some wealthy uncle who might have left them something. And maybe he did.

I clamber up on a railing and manage to glimpse the basilica a half mile away, massive and dignified at the far end of via della Conciliazione, a thin red foam of cardinals on the top stair, a tide of black behind them, presidents, queens, ambassadors, chancellors. Then come the descending parallels of streetlamps and a couple million bodies, like a beach of multicolored sand stretching all the way to the river. The air ripples; white media canopies, pitched on rooftops, flap against their tethers.

I think, If all the victims of the tsunami shuffled up a single boulevard, this is what it might look like. But this is more: 2 million, 3 million. Twice the population of Idaho. The numbers are too large to mean much until I am confronted with an entire city block of outhouses: at least a thousand of them, in three curving rows, bright blue, fans humming. A truck has somehow eased into their mass and sucks sewage out of the toilets, one after another.

Now there is applause, now singing. The song drifts from throats and radios and speaker towers. Someone up at the basilica begins a blessing, and practically everyone's face around me turns down. *Preghiamo.* Let us pray.

A cameraman on a scaffolding peels a banana. A priest in broken eyeglasses sleeps slumped against a tree trunk. A map of the earth, printed on a beach towel, is draped over his shoulders.

It's as if I've wandered into the biggest tailgate party in history, three days too long, the enthusiasm faded to a raw-throated, glassy fatigue—some people are crying; many are asleep. Volunteers hand out liters of water. A woman cradles a full-grown German shepherd. A man snores.

The blues of paramedics, the bright greens of volunteers, the navy pants and red pant-stripe of carabinieri— all the colors of Italy have turned out. Piazza Pia is closed; Borgo Sant'Angelo is closed. I will have to circumnavigate the entire state of the Vatican, I realize, only to end up where I started. All these somber faces, listening to their radios, staring at each other's back. If they're very tall, or lucky, all they can see is scaffolding, and cameras. Otherwise they're all looking at the back of someone else's head. And yet they're here, feeling that they're part of something.

I suddenly feel a bit proprietary about it—why is *my* access restricted? Who gave all these Polish flagbearers the right? And then I realize that this is the point—the papacy of John Paul, the Catholic Church, even Rome itself, belongs to anyone who is lucky enough to believe in it. This is medieval Catholicism: Rome at the hub of a vast and slowly revolving wheel, a cult of personality, a Metropolis of Church. Technology exposed every curve of John Paul's face to billions; he was the most familiar man in the world, your village pastor, your grandfather, your confessor, and the world is that much less consistent and safe without him.

The speakers sing again. The radios sing again. Maybe this right now is his final miracle: somehow he has transformed millions of spectators into millions of participants.

In the distance the great dome drifts in a tide of silver air, presiding over everything. This is the largest funeral in the history of the world, the largest gathering of dignitaries, and the largest single pilgrimage in the history of Christendom. For now it is dense, almost private. A woman pushes through the crowd, head down, wildflowers in both fists. Beside me a teenager with strands of barbed wire tattooed around his wrists wipes his eyes with the hem of his shirt. A nun on a suitcase gives me a smile. The slow singing starts and stops, and the men and women around me begin to respond to the mass, mumbling low in a smattering of languages. The sky blows past the cupola, hurrying, another April, the bright clouds moving as they've always moved above the events of this city, and 4 million voices rise to meet them.

꙰

Three days after the pope's funeral, Henry takes his first unaided steps. He pulls himself up by the front of the couch, stands a moment, rocking on his toes, then lets go. His little body staggers in a slow arc to the handle of a kitchen drawer six feet away. He hangs on, eyes wide, astonished at himself.

"Good!" Shauna shouts. "Good boy!"

All morning we sit on the floor in our pajamas and he walks between us, a sailor staggering across a deck in high seas, Owen watching from his blanket, smiling a confused smile.

The city slowly empties. Posters of John Paul saying *Grazie* or *Santo Subito* (Sainthood Now) remain pasted over Trastevere, but many of the Romans, at the market, in bars, are talking about *l'elezione*. The newspapers print diagrams of the Sistine Chapel, seating charts, profiles of all 134 voting cardinals. Our friend Steve Heuser, an editor for the *Boston Globe* living here for six months, starts sending home articles that include strange words such as *curia* (the Papal Court) and scrutineer (overseer of the ballots).

Black smoke, no pope. White smoke, new pope. Are those bells *the* bells? At the Academy, scholars host late-night seminars on papal succession. A betting pool to pick the new pope circulates. Myke Cuthbert, a musicologist, posts NCAA-style brackets on his apartment door. Cardinal Dionigi Tettamanzi of Italy is a high seed. Cardinal Oscar Andrés Rodríguez Maradiaga of Honduras is an

underdog. On the line marked winner, Myke has penciled
Duke.

Non-Catholics seem as interested in the conclave as
anyone: agnostics, Jews, gays, a Hindu friend writing
e-mails from back home—all beguiled by the screens of
secrecy, the eccentric vocabulary, the pomp and pageantry.
In 1274, Gregory X had the idea to lock all the cardinals
in a room. Sleep there, relieve yourself there, eat there.
One plate of food and one bowl of soup per day per man.
After five days of stalemating, this would be reduced to
bread, water, and wine. They couldn't draw an income,
couldn't communicate with the outside world. The proto-
col has hardly changed in 730 years.

"If cameras were allowed," our friend Janna says, "it'd
be the ultimate reality show."

Candlelight, a slow zoom on the host, a fresco rippling
with muscled *ignudi* out of focus behind him. "When we
come back, the most dramatic confrontation yet . . ."

Think of the political wrangling, the thousand infer-
ences reverberating beneath even the most simple
exchange. Whispers and fidelities, alliances, orthodoxies,
crimson robes sweeping down hallways and the swell of
the world's media straining against locked doors. Two
cardinals pause in a courtyard: a handshake, a sniffle, even
a half second of eye contact, and the mantle of power
drifts invisibly from one pair of shoulders to another.

Before his afternoon shift, Lorenzo the gatekeeper sits
with us in the garden behind the Academy, smiling at the
boys, letting Henry hold his finger as he walks laps
around his wooden chair. Henry cackles. Lorenzo says
there is an old Italian saying: "Always follow a fat pope
with a skinny pope."

Does that mean they'll follow a skinny pope with a fat one? In the betting pool I pick a sixty-nine-year-old German long shot named Karl Lehmann. I've never heard of him, but his photos display some serious jowls.

The boys fall and get back up, fall and get back up. Shauna takes a taxi to a doctor's appointment and I watch the babies alone. An hour into it, I'm ready to faint myself. There is a metaphor in all this standing up and falling over, I'm sure, but I'm too busy trying to keep their heads from smashing into the corners of tables to contemplate it.

The day the papal conclave meets for the first time, seven days after Henry took his first steps, Owen takes his. It is the most lovely afternoon I have seen in Rome, maybe the most lovely afternoon I have ever seen. Mounds of flowers perch atop trellises—dense racemes of wisteria hang everywhere. The lawns swirl with bees and the sky is radiant and flawless and resounds with gold; I feel as if I could tap it with a fingernail and set it ringing. "Look what sunshine," the nineteenth-century Roman poet Giuseppe Gioacchino Belli wrote, probably looking up into the sky above Trastevere on a day like this one. "Look: it's splitting the stones."

A cat sharpens his claws on a welcome mat. Sheets of miniature violets bloom in the garden walls, thirty feet above the ground.

Shauna sets Owen in the grass and stoops to pick up a toy, a few yards away. Suddenly Owen is there, having hauled himself up on the stroller and walked to her, his hands on the backs of her legs.

He grins. "Mo, mo?" he says. More, more. All afternoon we roam the lawn with our sons, stooped, our arms in a circle around their midsections, their little frames wobbling forward. They fall, they land on their palms. They stand up again.

Henry carries a bottle cap in each fist. Owen grins and grins. They rush headlong.

On the nineteenth of April, Shauna leaves the apartment to attend a talk at the Academy. I am helping the boys stack blocks. Across town, the cardinals tally their ballots and realize they have successfully elected a new pope. Smoke ascends from the chimney of the Sistine Chapel. *"Bianca, bianca,"* shout people in the piazza.

I know none of this—only that I need to change Henry's diaper, and Owen has given up on the blocks and is playing with the electrical cords beneath the diaper table. He has pulled the lamp onto the floor and has a section of the cord stuffed into his mouth when the sound of hundreds of clanging bells comes through the open window.

I check my watch: 6:08 p.m. Not a normal time for church bells.

I replace the lamp, change Henry's pants, pour milk into bottles, and wrestle the boys downstairs to the stroller. I wheel past the gate and call to the gatekeeper, Luca, "Is there a new pope?"

"Yes."

"Who is it?"

"There have only been the bells."

Only the bells. Stranded inside the Academy, poor Shauna, who has missed all the papal fanfare because she has been hospitalized, too busy with the boys, or too tired, is told the same thing. But the talk goes on, and she does not come down the front stairs.

I pivot the stroller and head past the Porta San Pancrazio and along the rim of the Janiculum. There is a faint, almost negligible rain. To my right the city is in shadow but off toward the west the sky is a rich yellow, and it feels as if any minute a half dozen rainbows will spring up.

I cut the switchbacks and plunge toward the Vatican. A bus passes, crammed full of nuns. The boys sing along with the bouncing of the stroller. I'm hurrying, but not too fast, and I don't see anyone really running. There seems to be more traffic than usual, speeding north, but it's hard to say for sure.

At one point, by the children's hospital, the traffic lets up and the boys stop singing and in the quiet I can hear bells ringing—thousands of them. It is a sound like every slumbering corner of the city waking up. And it's beautiful: the silvered light, St. Peter's dome wet and gleaming above the pines, the tiny drops of rain, Henry and Owen beaming, their hair flying back from the speed.

I wheel down the steep alley of Salita di Sant'Onofrio. The stroller thunks down the stairs. Now I see the people— all of them running in the same direction—slipping into the throat of via dei Penitenzieri. Literally a dozen people charge, without the usual Roman genius for jaywalking, right through the traffic. Brakes screech; no one pays any mind. Many are smiling big, authentic smiles. Men in suits, ladies holding hands—all of them are running. Several *motorini* squirt past us.

I, too, begin to jog, pushing the stroller. People walk out of restaurants, office buildings. It is not like the funeral—there are no cops, no civil service, no helicopters. There is no organization at all, yet everyone seems happy, peaceful.

When we reach it, St. Peter's Square is only perhaps half full. If I were alone, I could easily slip past the obelisk to the front of the crowd and put my hands on the railing beneath the main steps. Instead I end up positioning the stroller beneath the southern colonnade, between two of Bernini's massive pillars. I can peer around the end of a line of portable toilets and see big maroon curtains hanging in the central balcony on the façade of the basilica. I dig in the backpack we use for a diaper bag and find two stale quarters of a roll and hand them to the boys and hope I'm not too late. The crowd fills in behind us. Flags wave, people whisper. A toddler passing in front of us, towed by his mother, asks, *"Che cos'è, Mamma? Che cos'è?"* What is it, Mom?

Every minute the piazza packs in tighter. Over my shoulder is the now familiar sight of hundreds of lights on the media scaffolding just off the Largo del Colonnato. Men in suits face the glare, holding microphones, their backs to the piazza. Rows of men in darker suits stand on top of the colonnade itself, below the papal apartments, security probably. A whole retinue of Swiss Guards stands at attention in their harlequin colors at the base of the basilica steps.

We have been there maybe three minutes when the curtains shift. A murmur rolls through the crowd. A man steps out in a red skullcap and leans into a microphone and says, "Brothers and sisters," in Italian. Then he says, *"Habemus Papam."* We have a pope.

I clap, along with everyone, and the applause dies down and he says something else, maybe more Latin, and the crowd roars—absolutely *roars*—and the twins burst into tears.

The cardinal retreats and some helpers show up and drop a gilded carpet, big as an Olympic swimming pool, over the railing and secure it and move back inside. The curtains fall still once again. I take the boys out of the stroller one at a time and try to calm them. The drizzle remains faint. The swirling cloudscape behind St. Peter's flushes with light.

Ceremony is story. Blood beats in the temples, eyes stop blinking, a delicate silence rises and stretches, and the white-hot center of the world's attention pauses momentarily along its insatiable sweep. All the faces around me—a man standing on the pedals of his bicycle, a middle-aged woman with gigantic pearl earrings, a touch of empire about her shoulders—are strikingly earnest. Are we here because we want to know who will become pope? Or are we here out of vanity—because we want to be able to say we were here? Both, of course. The Church is making narrative, and this is the story's climactic moment. Right now we're here mostly because we want to know what will happen next, because we're most of the way through a rich and complicated story. The curtain is up, the orchestra is playing; this is the thrill of drama and the Catholic Church is the most experienced dramatist in the world.

Before any outcome, before cynicism, or disappointment, or exultation—there is hope, and the promise of change. The joy is in the expectancy, in the swelling potential of it all. The last-second shot hangs above the rim; the final ballot box is upended onto the counting table. It's the admissions envelope in the mailbox, the corner of the telegraph slip sticking out from under the door. It's Christmas morning, it's holding the pregnancy test to the light. It's springtime.

Not-knowing is always more thrilling than knowing. Not-knowing is where hope and art and possibility and invention come from. It is not-knowing, that old, old thing, that allows everything to be renewed.

I whisper to Henry what I see: the halberds of the Swiss Guards, the heavy tapestries. A pigeon lands on the rim of a fountain and rests, panting. Dozens of cardinals in brilliant scarlet emerge on two flanking balconies on the façade of the basilica. Then the maroon curtain shifts on the central balcony and the crowd howls and the boys start screaming again: screaming into the roar, the future, the unknown. The noise is such that, two feet away, I cannot hear their cries.

"Here he comes," I tell Henry.

A man steps out. His arms are raised. A blessing? A sign of victory? He is tiny beneath the towering curtains. He wears white, with a black stole, and seems to be bareheaded. Indeed, by far the most striking thing about him is his hair: it is a dazzling, beautiful white.

He is the 266th pope since Simon Peter took the reins from Jesus in AD 32. A cardinal holds out a microphone. The new pope licks his lips, the light sets his hair on fire. He turns his head a few degrees to his right, and my sons—their little stroller, wedged between two pillars— are directly in his line of sight.

His arms drop; the roar dies. He says a sentence or two that includes John Paul II's name and the roar surges back up, loud enough to set the old pillars reeling, a roar that is the sum of thousands of individual voices but somehow more than that, too. By now the twins are inconsolable.

Who is it? I tap the shoulder of a man with the ear-buds of a portable radio in his ears.

"The German."

"Ratzenburger?"

Carefully, and clearly annoyed, he says, *"Ratzinger,"* and puts his earphone back in.

"Ahhh," I say, but this means little to me. For now it doesn't matter, anyway. I squeeze the stroller through the crowd and back onto the street and unstrap the boys beside the entrance to a restaurant and hold them until they're calm.

People are still rushing past us, hurrying toward the show, many looking deeply happy, as if they have escaped the weights of their bodies, a nun running with a pig-tailed girl holding each of her hands, three small priests jogging behind them, smiling immensely. From here, a block away, the church is soaked in light. Rays of sun sift past the cupola. The crowd is a field of color through the fat, white stripes of the colonnade.

Every story seeks, in Emerson's words, the "invisible and imponderable." Faith, loss, emotional contact. But to get there, oddly enough, the storyteller must use the visible, the physical, the eminently tangible: the reader, first and foremost, must be convinced. And details—the right details in the right places—are what do the convincing. The ringing mouth of a 9-ton bell, green with verdigris, shows itself, then sweeps away again. A gilded carpet unfurls from a balcony. Two three-story curtains ripple, then part. A man steps into the light.

The glory of architecture, the puffing chimney, the starched white robe—these details are carefully chosen; they are there to reinforce majesty, divinity, to assure us that what is said to be happening actually is happening.

And doesn't a writer do the same thing? Isn't she knitting together scraps of dreams? She hunts down the most vivid details and links them in sequences that will let a reader see, smell, and hear a world that seems complete in itself; she builds a stage set and painstakingly hides all the struts and wires and nail holes, then stands back and hopes whoever might come to see it will believe.

As I work on yet another draft of my story, I try to remember these lessons. A journal entry is for its writer; it helps its writer refine, perceive, and process the world. But a story—a finished piece of writing—is for its reader; it should help its *reader* refine, perceive, and process the world—the one particular world of the story, which is an invention, a dream. A writer manufactures a dream. And each draft should present a version of that dream that is more precisely rendered and more consistently sustained than the last.

Every morning I try to remind myself to give unreservedly, to pore over everything, to test each sentence for fractures in the dream.

Five days after Cardinal Ratzinger is elected, he is installed as Pope Benedict XVI. Shauna and I push the stroller through Trastevere in the drizzle. The old pope is buried, the new one is draped in gold, and meanwhile the city looks like an empty theater, uniformed ushers walking about with their dustpans, quietly sweeping up.

In overcast light, on a Sunday afternoon, Rome can look especially bleak, storefronts shuttered and tagged with graffiti, iron bars across ground-floor windows. On via Ippolito Nievo, near a toy store we sometimes visit, a burst water main has floated trash across an entire block: plastic bags, banana peels, shredded paper, a million colorless scraps of cardboard. Trash is clotted over storm drains, slung limply across the gutters, collected in puddles under parked cars. A mechanized street sweeper howls in front of us.

In the Forum archaeologists crouch in their pits with their buckets and trowels and brushes, tweezering away the clay. Nearby, restorers clamp scaffolding to yet another church façade. Try for a moment to understand how overwhelmingly many dimpled and cracking surfaces this city must try to keep clean: fonts, flower petals, pediments, railings, hieroglyphics on obelisks, the furrowed robes of ten thousand solemn Madonnas, and the plump cheeks of a hundred thousand grinning cherubs. We all fight our daily battles with entropy—deadhead the tulips, pick up the fallen Cheerios, carry out the used diapers—but Rome has it the worst. It is a Metropolitan Museum of Art the size of Manhattan, no roof, no display cases, and half a million combustion engines rumbling in the hallways.

If you average it out over the millennia, the detritus has piled up over Rome at somewhere near an inch a year. Hadrian would have entered the Pantheon by *climbing* stairs. Now we have to brake the stroller as we coast down toward it. The four smashed temples in Largo di Torre

Argentina, once on pedestals in the open light, are now about thirty feet below the level of today's sidewalk. You need a *permesso* and a stepladder to descend to them. By the fifteenth century, Nero's monstrous pleasure palace, the Domus Aurea, had become a series of underground caverns lived in by shepherds. Supposedly Raphael and Pinturicchio would rappel into the rooms and study the frescoes by torchlight.

All around us the streets continue to rise imperceptibly: chewing gum, bird droppings, leaf litter, skin cells, gelato spoons, particles of exhaust, bits of buildings, shreds of insect wings, the exhalations of lovers and the castings of earthworms—a ghostly compost raining ceaselessly onto the city. Ancient Romans stripped the Apennines of trees, and Renaissance Romans did it again, and ever since the spring rains have pulled the soil off the mountains and spread it across the plains. Every minute here the graves of the dead sink a fraction deeper. You can't help but wonder what frescoes, what stonework, what sconces and dinnerware, lie entombed beneath your shoes.

In two thousand more years, maybe everything Pope Benedict can see from his apartment window will be a hundred feet underground.

Water gurgles through the gutters. Henry and Owen kick at their rain shield. The billion nightcrawlers of Rome swim beneath us, leaving their castings, navigating the oceans of the past.

May brings more wind: the sky blown clean, the cornices of the palaces electric with light. House martins dive-bomb gaps in the shutters of the Academy building and clamber into hidden nests and keep scholars in their little apartments awake half the night.

All Henry and Owen want to do is walk, and all they do when they walk is wipe out. Bruises flare and fade on their bodies like storm clouds: one at the bridge of Henry's nose yellowing as one on Owen's right temple darkens and swells. At the far end of the terrace, Owen plucks a petal off a tulip and staggers in a slow circle and finally holds it out—a bright yellow panel of silk—to his brother.

In the Villa Sciarra the peacocks strut in their cage and the cypresses seethe and three women stroll past, each with a macaw on her right shoulder. One of the women is rubbing her bird's wing and saying, *"Qui siamo, qui siamo,"* here we are, here we are, over and over.

No brain tumors, no blood clots. Shauna's test results are fine. Her doctor flushes wax out of her ears and tells her to keep hydrated. We celebrate by deciding to leave the boys with Tacy for an entire day—morning to evening— while we take the train to Spoleto, a hill town in Umbria.

We say good-bye, step through the front gate. The sky is a jeweled blue. We swing the trash into the Dumpster. A taxi hauls us past the Vittoriano, down via Nazionale, BMWs and Fiats racing beside us, faces fluttering past like sheets of paper, *motorini* clicking across the cobbles, the riders often so close, even at thirty miles an hour, that I could reach out the window and tap their thighs.

The train station, Termini, swarms with travelers—it is part homeless shelter/part mall—but it feels serene to us; we can hardly believe how unencumbered we are: two

sweaters, two small backpacks. A pair of sunglasses, a bottle of water. No baby wipes, no milk cartons, no teething
toys. To be a parent and take an occasional day off from
being a parent is a special kind of joy—a lightening, a
sweetness made sweeter by its impermanence.

We buy tickets, find our seats. The weeds between
adjacent tracks are a vivid, almost tropical green. The
train starts forward and the thousand switches of Termini
glide past above the windows. In a minute we're in the
suburbs, rooftops studded with TV antennas, the back of
a supermarket, a depot for wounded buses, an overpass, a
slice of aqueduct, two moldering temples wearing a haze
of new growth.

Then we're out: ilex and oak, the stripe of a highway,
and the distant swell of a mountain draped with clouds.
Telephone wires race alongside, dashing in shallow
parabolas from pole to pole. I think of Henry and Owen,
so curious about the world—yesterday they staggered
down the gravel paths in the Villa Sciarra, the trees above
them bursting with flowers. "Daadadaada," sang Owen.
Henry tried for half a minute to grasp a piece of gravel
between his thumb and his forefinger.

In Spoleto we climb into the old town from the train
station and eat candy bars on a fourteenth-century bridge
built on 250-foot-high stone arches. A cloud blows through
the gorge and engulfs us in a light drizzle and moves on,
floating down the valley, shot through with light. Spires
of smoke rise from fields. The wind smells of honey-
suckle, then wild rose, then turned earth. A rainbow—
no kidding—threads halfway across the gorge and touches
the quilts of olive groves below town.

Shauna smiles and breaks into a run; her cheeks glow

pink. We wander through the duomo; we lie on our backs on a bench and trade pages of a newspaper. In the afternoon we choose an entryway at random and clamber into a velvety, cramped restaurant, waiters in tuxedos, lamps turned low.

What we eat is a poem.

Campanella soffiata alla caciottina locale con fonduta di parmigiano e tartufo nero; strengozzi alla Spoletina con pomodori, peperoncino, pecorino e prezzemolo; lombello di maialino in rete di lardo della Valnerina, salsa delicata al pecorino e pere al rosso di Montefalco; e sformatino caldo al cioccolato con crema all'arancia.

Blown campenalla (ruffled-edge pasta) with local sheep's milk cheese, topped with Parmesan and black truffle fondue; Spoleto-style strengozzi (to call these dumplings is akin to calling a Rolls-Royce a golf cart) with tomatoes, peperoncino, pecorino cheese, and parsley; the loin of a Valnerina piglet in a pecorino, pear, and Montefalco red-wine sauce; and a hot, wet chocolate flan smothered with orange cream.

We close our eyes; we slide the forks out of our mouths. "It's ridiculous," Shauna says.

At dusk the plains below town turn blue, the sky indigo. We fall into train seats sunburned and happy. Every minute a tunnel flashes past, sucking the air out of our ears.

I open a book. Shauna closes her eyes. The city rushes toward us. Someday, I tell her, we'll come back to Spoleto and sleep a night in the Hotel Gattapone, built into a cliffside, and cross that fourteenth-century bridge at dusk and walk the muddy trail that winds across the far side of the gorge to a picnic table above a ruined hermitage and drink a bottle of wine and eat pecorino cheese and walk back across the bridge in the full dark beneath the four naked bulbs, spaced a hundred feet apart, and our sons will run out in front of us.

The dreams of parents. Our reflection shines in the train windows. Occasionally the darkness is broken by a distant town, its yellow lights riding the crest of a hill in the distance.

SUMMER

DAYS LIKE THIS: THE MOST FLAWLESS BLUE YOU could imagine, every leaf edged with gold. Tiny strawberries fatten in the garden and awnings flap and there are the big oceangoing sighs of the umbrella pines. The Academy and its fellows become like adolescent summer campers, cooped, artists trampling on scholars, scholars trampling on artists; they post tirades on the bulletin boards about misuse of Academy vans; the upstairs kitchen smells of spilled milk, garlic, and intrigue.

If you pause in the street, you can feel the sunlight pounding your shoulders. It is as if every day the sun gains slightly more mass. Shauna collects the boys from their naps and their shirts are soaked. By afternoon Owen's little bathroom has become a broiling suffocation chamber.

Only early mornings remain cool. Wall lizards creep across the terrace, with neon backs and delicate toes and long tails like slips of shadow. Tiny red mites swarm beneath the potted tulips. I lift a pot and a city of mites erupts into activity.

As I walk to my studio, there is a dawning sense of the temporariness of this life. In two months we will be cast out of the Academy, and George the sculptor will have to pack up his meticulous plaster bowls, and the bristling and sharpened and painted forest in Jon Piasecki's studio will disappear. By late August, the door of practically every studio I pass on the way to work will have a different name fixed to it. Mine included.

We decide to visit Umbria every Wednesday for the rest of the weeks we're in Italy. In May we crisscross the vale of Spoleto, spend a Wednesday in Todi, a Wednesday in Orvieto, a Wednesday in Assisi. We step off the train into daydreams—no schedules, no grappling with writing, our children back in the city, dozing away, and here are the cramped, contorted alleys and distant gorges and sudden archways and painted shutters and always the burnishing, majestic light and the azure distances. Geraniums spill from window boxes, eyes peep at us from shadowed doorways. We climb onto the ramparts of town walls and wind pours through our shirts and sends leaves, or great flexing clouds of pollen, or—once—a rectangle of paper with a drawing of a face on it spinning past us, flying out over the rooftops. In restaurants I convince myself I can taste that wind in the wine, and the herbs, and especially in the oil.

Assisi is alive with chimney swifts—the air above the piazzas are snowstorms of birds, swirling over the rooftops at dusk like reef fish. To avoid tourists there, all one has to do is climb: two blocks above the cathedral, the streets are dead quiet and the houses cling to slopes and the vale far below fades imperceptibly into twilight.

The alleys in Orvieto on a rainy afternoon smell like old basements: cisterns, old paper, and must. Orvieto, we learn, has a mirror city running beneath its streets, miles of

subterranean galleries and crypts and cellars, pickax basements, forgotten quarries, so many tunnels nobody knows
how extensive they are.

In Todi, we enter a chapel through a side door and are
suddenly in the middle of twenty nuns, all praying silently;
the only sounds the sliding of zippers on prayer books.

We visit Giotto's famous frescoes in Assisi, most
remarkable for their breathtaking blues: a pigment he
made by grinding lapis lazuli into a powder, horrifyingly
expensive; he reserved blue for only the loveliest skies, the
holiest robes.

On the façade of the duomo in Orvieto, the thirteenth-
century sculptor Lorenzo Maitani has carved seemingly
half the books of the Bible into vertical slabs of marble.
Eve appears to physically step from Adam's rib. Cain pre-
pares to give Abel a solid pounding with a sledgehammer.
Maitani has made trees lacy as coral; serpents coiling out
of walls; devils rending faces. During the Last Judgment,
whole tangles of tormented bodies spill from the stone.

The volcanic tuff in every town possesses a slightly different hue: burnt yellow, faded pink, dirty blue. Little
black scorpions wander into shoes and beetles crawl in
bathtubs and boars rumble across driveways. Cyclamen
send runners of color through the forests. Between train
tracks, poppies on skinny stems—bright red splashes of
paint—buck in the wake of the trains. To return to Rome
is to return exhilarated and windburned and unclenched,
but always a bit sad, too, to see the *motorini* and billboards,
to slip back inside the walls, to leave behind so much distance and color and sky.

Toward the end of May I walk into the little grocery store, Beti, after living in Rome for nine months and say good afternoon to the same exact woman from whom I once demanded grapefruit sauce and ask her in Italian for a loaf of bread, two hamburger rolls, an apple muffin, three-tenths of a kilogram of pizza *bianca,* and a can of tuna fish, and I don't screw up a single syllable.

What happens? I get my groceries. No streamers drop from the ceiling, no strobe lights start flashing. The grocer doesn't reach across the counter and take my face in her hands and kiss me on the forehead.

You communicated. So what. Go pay at the register.

No, instead she asks me something in quick-fire Italian about Henry and Owen, something about their hair, but she speaks so quickly that I miss 80 percent of it and sheepishly, stepping down from my throne of fluency, have to ask, "I'm sorry, more slowly, please?"

On the second of June, the Feast of the Republic, fifty-nine years since Italians voted to replace monarchy with democracy, Romans celebrate by lining the via dei Fori Imperiali between the Vittoriano and the Colosseum to watch tanks and a police Lamborghini and a World War II torpedo on a flatbed come rolling past. Next come carabinieri with drums and swords, infantry in berets, even a regiment of cheerleaders swishing white pom-poms. For a finale, nine antitank jets scream in formation over the Vittoriano, spewing white and green and red smoke.

That night we wake to fireworks launching off the roof of the villa across the street. Sparks and smoke below the trees, a whistle, an explosion, then sparks and smoke above the trees. Shauna and I stand at the terrace door blinking away sleep. Any moment the boys will wake up and start screaming. The street flares blue, white, red. Funny how to celebrate peace we seem to want to simulate war.

Fifty-nine is a recurring number. There have been fifty-nine different Italian governments since World War II. Media magnate Silvio Berlusconi's current government will be the first postwar administration to stay in power for a full term. And yet the Italians walk about in the summer heat as if drugged, as if patience is the one quality they possess in spades.

Here's another line from the poet Belli: "I'm not myself when I exert myself."

At our favorite restaurant we eat hopelessly good antipasti: tiny roasted tomatoes; fried slips of zucchini thin as tissue paper; crisp and wet green beans; grilled bell peppers. Then we share a chicken pounded with salt and peppercorns and roasted on hot stones. We finish our meal in maybe two hours and wait another hour and a half for the bill. I try pleases, I point to my watch and say, *"la babysitter . . ."*

"Va bene," the waiter says. Okay. No problem. Still, we wait thirty more minutes. It comes when it comes. As if the waiters are trying to teach us something.

One afternoon, walking down via Carini to buy milk, we pass the Banca di Roma and its goateed, pistol-wearing guard, when I notice, for the first time, the window decal that displays the banking hours.

Mornings: 8.30–11.30.
Afternoons: 14.15–15.40.
Closed Saturdays.

The bank is open less than four and a half hours a day. Inside, customers sit hip to hip, clutching slips of paper, attention on a big LED number, another eye of God.

This coming Sunday will be the first "ecological Sunday" of the summer, meaning gas-powered vehicles are prevented from circulating in Trastevere or the historic center from 10 a.m. to 6 p.m. Of course, two miles away, the 50th Annual Rome Motor Show will be held at the Foro Italico, ten thousand cars, and models in Altieri dresses, and all those engines running all weekend long.

I finish my short story about the flooded village. It is nine thousand words; it has taken me almost six months to write. It is the first piece of fiction I have completed since the boys were born. I put it in the mail for New York and drink a half a bottle of Chianti and fall asleep reading Pliny's account of giant blue worms in the Ganges River. "They are so strong," he writes, "that they carry off elephants coming to drink by gripping the trunk in their teeth."

I wake at 3 a.m., sweating. Owen is crying in his crib. His room is sweltering. I lie with him on the couch and drift in and out of nightmares, his little weight on my chest, the morning sweeping relentlessly toward us, dawn flowing across the Black Sea, touching Bulgaria. Soon people in apartments in Yugoslavia will be starting their days; then the Croatians, then the Umbrians. Then it'll be our turn.

By now, mid-June, even dawn is hot. Thick ceilings of clouds clamp in the heat. At night I try keeping the windows open, but then the *motorini* keep me up, and the mosquitoes come for Shauna. I try shutting the windows but then the air gathers so much weight it feels as if I've sealed us inside a plastic bag.

The following night Owen wakes crying at 2, 3, 4, 5, and 6 a.m. I bring him milk, I rock him. I feel myself reentering the familiar country of insomnia—the ghostly hours, the slow thoughts, the inability to put together clear sentences.

"He's getting molars," Shauna says. "Poor guy." He sucks a stale corner of pizza *bianca* on the terrace. I try to imagine sprouting big, round pieces of skeleton through my gums.

In the afternoons we walk stultified through the city, sky throbbing, stroller tires rubbery on the cobbles, the axles flexing, as if the metal is softening and the whole contraption might collapse. I carry along a notebook but hardly manage to open it; the heat is like having my brain removed and a bunch of hot, wet cotton stuffed behind my eyes. My skin slumps; my limbs go heavy. I daydream but nothing is happening in my head—I'm merely staring into the world, seeing blankness.

"We can't escape it," I hear Shauna say into the phone one evening. "Cannot get away from it." Diaper rashes creep up the boys' chests and backs. Still, their enthusiasm for the world astounds. Everything—a roll of tape, a telephone jack, each other's hair—warrants investigation. Whoever says adults are better at paying attention than children is wrong: we're too busy filtering out the world, focusing on some task or another, paying *no* attention. Our kids are the ones discovering new continents all day long. Sometimes, looking at them, I feel as if Henry and Owen live permanently in that resplendent, taut state of awareness that we adults only reach when our cars are sliding on ice through a red light, or our airplane is thudding through turbulence.

My own attention is sucked ceaselessly toward water. The Tiber, sure, but the Tiber is too slow and too brown, sliding past without a ripple; in this weather it hardly seems like water at all. It's the fountains: drinking fountains, district fountains, monumental fountains. A travel website says there are 280 fountains in Rome, but it seems as if there are more: the tower of miters and keys that is the Fontanella delle Tiare in the Borgo; the giant twin bathtubs in Piazza Farnese; the lions spewing water in Piazza San Bernardo. There is a spigot spilling day and night into a stone tank at the bottom of via di Porta San Pancrazio; another beside our bus stop; another near Garibaldi's huge statue atop the Janiculum.

Passing the turtle fountain in the Jewish quarter, in murderous sunlight, I watch a man sitting on its railing undress an apple with a penknife, turning the apple like a table leg in a router, the skin curling off in a single, green spiral. When he is done, he sets the coil of skin on the stair beside him, reaches back, and washes his blade in the water.

My favorites are not the dramatic fountains, the arcing shooters, the twin jets in front of St. Peter's, or the pomp and roar of the Fontanone. The best fountains are the pensive dribblers, the bubblers, the brimming basins, the damp backs of nymphs and centaurs, the petrified grotesquerie of Villa Sciarra. The little burbling pinecone in Piazza Venezia. Remove them and there is no present tense, no circulatory system, no dreams to balance the waking hours. No Rome.

I sit with a notebook and watch the tides of people come and go, a time-lapse of an afternoon, blurs of darkness roiling through the light, crossing paths, intersecting energies, the fountains in the piazzas pouring on and on. Before these medieval houses were plumbed, every time you wanted to wash your shirts or vegetables or children, you had to march to the basin in front of your home. Think how often you'd see friends, enemies, the neighbor girl you'd fallen in love with. Think of the perpetual trickle of gossip, the hanging mists of rumor. These were the original office watercoolers.

Ancient Romans had their baths, of course, colossal and preposterous, big as Umbrian hill towns. The Baths of Caracalla alone covered twenty-seven acres. The Baths of Diocletian were larger, almost twice as large as the nineteen-acre White House complex of gardens and buildings in Washington, D.C. You worked till noon, you wandered over to the baths with your bottle of olive oil and skin-scraper: warm pool, hot pool, finish with a cold rinse.

At the end of the Empire, Roman aqueducts brought 1,747,000 cubic meters of water into the city every day. With a population just shy of one million, that amounted to 461.5 gallons per person. Every day.

One ninety-degree afternoon, Shauna and I stop by the northern fountain in Piazza Navona, not Bernini's huge Fountain at the Four Rivers, but the Fountain of Neptune, the naked sea god poised to sink a spear into a serpent that has coiled a tentacle around his thigh. The basin has been drained. A couple of city workers in jumpsuits scrub the marble with nylon push brooms. Hoses lie fat and listless on the cobbles. *"Buongiorno,"* we say, but they

hardly nod. Everything is withered: dark smears in Neptune's back muscles, pigeon shit on the nymphs, and it
seems as if this end of the piazza has somehow faded, too.
No flush; no sparkle. No children, no laughter; the
awnings of the cafés hardly flutter; it is as if history is seep-
ing out of the stones, clogging the air, stifling everything.

But soon enough the fountain is refilled, the pump
begins to churn, innocence rinses away experience, present
overwhelms past, the corpse reanimates. Rome lives again.

By evening, in this heat, the whole city twists into a
whirlpool: the humidity, the marshy odor of the Tiber,
gasoline fumes swirling in an alley, the clinking of distant
tableware—in a Roman dusk in summer you can stare at
a fountain and see nothing, feel nothing, all existence
reduced to the suspension of water at the apex of its
ascent, delayed a millisecond, flooded with light, just
before it begins its fall. It is a state to chase after.

Wherever you might be right now, water—the ceaseless hydrant in the Campo dei Fiori, Bernini's grand old
leaking boat in Piazza di Spagna—circulates through this
ancient city, thrumming through its arteries, beating in its
hearts. Even the engulfing mess of the Trevi Fountain,
with its gaggles and trinket barkers and hundred thousand blackened gum circles and fluorescent galaxy of
crushed gelato spoons between the cobbles, is somehow
essential. It is flushing, always flushing.

We lean over the rail; we hurl pennies at the gods.

I search three department stores until I find an inflatable
pool and bring it back to the apartment and blow it up on
the terrace. We upend a couple of warm pitchers into it

and lower the boys in. Owen squeals with delight, splashing, rolling a ball back and forth. Henry tenses, his little body motionless. He does not cry, but he does not move either. Eventually, without disturbing anything around him, ignoring Owen's shrieks and splashes, he begins to carefully pour water back and forth from the interior of one LEGO into the interior of another.

Shauna begins keeping our shutters closed around the clock. They are aluminum and black, and by noon the sun has heated the south-facing ones to the point where we can no longer touch them. The city is drugged with heat; the stones are dead; the streets devastatingly quiet. From one until four, no one moves. Shutters are drawn, storefronts sealed—it might as well be 3 a.m. I give the Roman siesta a try, lying on top of the bedsheet, but it's hopeless. I sweat; little strings of worry pull through my brain, conjectures, to-do lists. I get up, move through the apartment in a gray twilight, reading novels, writing in my journal, stripes of sun blazing between the shutter slats.

Who could write a book in this? How did Pliny do it? From what I can tell, summer pushes Romans to the edges, mornings and evenings, suburbs and summer homes. In the city center, in the heat of a summer afternoon, churches are the only refuges, dim and cool, spots swarming across the floors, the paintings black and impossible, the altars dwarfed beneath dusty chandeliers, tour groups shuffling down gloomy lanes of pillars. I want to stay in these churches for hours; I want to take off my shirt and lie on the marble, my chest against the stone, and let the perpetual dusk drift over me.

Instead I steal mint from the Academy garden and crush it in glasses with sugar and rum, and we sit with friends on our terrace drinking and soaking our feet in the baby pool.

Halfway through June we return from a tiny hill town called Narni, one more Wednesday in Umbria. Rain streaks the train windows and the headlines say, *Blood on the Umbrian Highway: 2 Dead*. But maybe I'm mistranslating, because two truck drivers burned to death in an alpine tunnel near Turin yesterday, 630 kilometers away. Maybe drivers are dying in pairs all over Italy.

Mosquitoes travel the aisles. A shack in a field flashes past, a dark-faced man staring across a table made from a sheet of corrugated iron. The Tiber appears, green and slow, fringed with plastic bags. Then it's gone. Shauna sleeps beside me, hands folded. Ahead of us, only a few miles away, our boys chase Tacy around the apartment. The train slows as it rattles into Tiburtina, the last stop before Termini.

The underside of a bridge coasts past, lacquered with graffiti. Graffiti wraps every available surface of an uncoupled train car, even the windows. *TYSON,* says the back of a supermarket, and, *Chiamate subito Rambo,* which means "Call Rambo immediately." I pick out *Onion!* and *Piantatela* (Stop it). For every legible scribble, a hundred are illegible, swirls and loops, drastic, hyper-stylized tags.

I think of home: Idaho in mid-June, the high meadows seething with flowers, sagebrush blooming, streams roaring. Even in the valley, in Boise, the heat won't have set in yet, and the nights will be long and cool and unblemished.

But here, in this heat, everything feels sticky and worn, overvisited, overexamined. Everything feels as if it were written on. Monuments, windows, trash cans, awnings, and rocks. Ankles, backs, shoulders. You see it most obviously from the trains, as you leave behind the gorges and groves of the countryside and enter the apartment blocks and body shops, slipping beneath overpasses and tension wires, the horizon progressively shrinking. More people here, more paint. Nations of tourists padding through the streets. *Stop Bush, Febo, TASMO. Magik, Els, DMG don't touch.*

An article the other day said Roman authorities spend €2.5 million (about $3 million) a year scrubbing 4.25 million square meters of graffiti off city walls. This cannot approach what private-property owners must spend. On a dozen different mornings I've seen sad-looking men taking water and steel wool and some dreadful solvent to the bricks of their restaurants. The street level of nearly every wall in the city center is paler than the rest, scrubbed and bleached and repainted a dozen times. Then tagged again: *Panda7, Dumbo, Satan!* Subway trains are sometimes so thoroughly covered they become montages of color: greens and reds and blues, conduits of paint bellowing through the labyrinth.

Kung has been busy in Trastevere. So has *Uncle Festah.* On via Nazionale, a single tow-zone sign sports maybe ten surfing stickers along with *Fuck Cops, Rex,* and *Real Rock,* all in English. A stenciled marijuana leaf has been applied maybe a hundred times along a block of via Cavour.

No Blood for Oil is rampant. So are *No War* and *Nè USA, nè Islam! (Neither USA, nor Islam)* and *USA GO AWAY*. Laura's children come home from school and ask her if *Yankee Go Home* means what they think it means.

Hammers and sickles, swastikas, pentagrams, anarchy *A*'s. The wall above the doorbell of a government agency has been labeled *Assassini*. A window shutter nearby reads *Tetti per tutti* (Roofs for everyone).

Even the seemingly innocuous slogan is usually at least tangentially political: *Me ne frego* (I don't give a damn) was the motto of Mussolini's paramilitary groups, the Blackshirts. *Carlo vive* (Carlo lives) is a reference to Carlo Giuliani, a twenty-three-year-old demonstrator who was killed by police during the 2001 G-8 summit in Genoa.

The pearls are often in mishandled English: *Punk Rains; Einstein Rules Relatively OK?;* and *Always let you guides by love.*

My favorite is near the Trevi Fountain: *Viva Nixon.*

They've been doing it forever here. There is graffiti over two thousand years old in the ancient port city of Ostia. Lava preserved a bunch of it at Pompeii. In the Palatine Museum, there's a first-century drawing of Christ on the cross with an ass's head. Several meters below the altar at St. Peter's, second-century pilgrims put their tags on what is believed to be Peter's grave.

There was the medieval graffiti I saw inside Trajan's column. Our friend Janna tells me that in 1528, a German invader scratched *Why wouldn't I laugh? The Lansquenets* [German soldiers] *have made the pope flee* above a fresco in the Villa Farnesina down in Trastevere. Chapel singers signed their names into the lofts of the Sistine Chapel, and Napoléon's soldiers got busy on the walls at Villa

Madama. The legendary architect/etcher Piranesi scribbled *Piranesi 1741* into a grotto at Hadrian's Villa with a red crayon.

Who am I to judge? I've put my name here and there. We all mark our spaces somehow. The smell of aerosol, the satisfying sound of a ball bearing rattling in a tall can: in a city where private grinds ceaselessly against public, maybe paint helps define boundaries.

Even Umbria—which looks wild in places—is touched, and touched everywhere: the fraying spire of smoke from a farmer's burn pile, the bright cliffs of quarries, the pine forest drifting past our train window that I realize, after a moment, is planted in rows.

Natives, exotics: even the umbrella pine, symbol of Rome, known to many as the Italian pine, may not be an indigenous plant—some believe that the Etruscans brought it from the Middle East. But should a botanist continue to call a tree exotic if it has been growing and dying here for over three thousand years?

When we get homesick, it is not so much for undubbed movies or Ziploc bags or turkey sandwiches as it is for landscapes, the beige hills and long-drawn skies of Idaho. In Boise no swirling convolutions of ancient cities hide beneath the streets, no empires lurk beneath the weeds. Just quiet houses, familiar faces.

Our train shunts through the maze of rails funneling into Termini. Rain hisses on the roof. A final quarter-mile of graffiti slinks past. *Rex* and *SLIM* and *Up! Up!* Shauna and I shoulder our bags and move down the aisle and hold hands as we climb back out into the city.

On the night of the summer solstice men walk up and down both banks of the Tiber, lighting 2,758 pan candles, one for every year since Rome's founding. If I squint, I can look upriver from the Garibaldi bridge in Trastevere at two arcing smears of light, the reflections wrinkling and settling on the water, like those long-exposure photographs of skiers cruising down lightless slopes holding torches.

I walk the city in the darkness, sleepy but unable to sleep, circling the Palatine, first of Rome's Seven Hills. The skeletons of ruined palaces are ghostly against the sky. A campanile hovers. Hidden in grassy mounds up there, the first cicadas practice their songs. A few weeks from now they'll be roaring.

Up here, late at night, the city seems to exhale, one protracted outpouring of breath: a distant voice from a balcony, tailpipes, wind in the trees. Sighs, wingbeats, a meandering static. Maybe, maybe—although I haven't heard one all year—a rooftop nightingale. Time devours everyone—Romulus, Pliny the Elder, John Keats, John Paul II—but tonight it feels as if some faint dispersal of them lingers, a tone, a shade, the vast accumulation of souls.

The city breathes out into the countryside and the breath diffuses and the silence out there tries to absorb it. Up on the Janiculum my little one-year-olds breathe in their beds, inhaling, exhaling.

From the locked gate at the Clivo di Venere Felice, with the Forum dark and quiet behind me, the wedge of the Colosseum I can see up ahead is webbed in spotlights, a vast and lonely specter, frozen in the glare, one streamer of ivy waving gently back and forth. Even now, after midnight, its tourists—small and fatigued—walk their laps.

Insomnia: I paddle toward sleep; sleep recedes beyond the horizon. It is as if thousands of tiny wires have been torn out of my neck. Italian tongue twisters corkscrew through my ears: *Pelè partì parà per il Perù, però perì per il purè.* Pelè left for Peru a paratrooper, but perished as puree. *Pio Pietro Paolo Pula, pittore Palermitano, pinse pittura per poco prezzo.* Pio Pietro Paolo Pula, painter from Palermo, paints a painting for a pittance.

I walk the boys to the vegetable stand on a Saturday morning, my brain a miasma: a *pesca* is peach, a *pesce* is a fish. Peaches, plural, are *pesche. Pizza* is pizza but a *pezzo* is a piece, a *pozzo* is a well, *pezze* are patches, and a *pazzo* is a nutcase. A *puzza* is a stench: Shauna sings, *Puzza, puzza,* to Henry while she changes his diaper.

When you're overheated, worn out, and surrounded by Italians, the poetry that is their language can quickly slide toward gibberish. *Buongiorno* becomes *wan journey;* prices become nursery rhymes. One hundred and eighty-eight is *centottantotto.* Five hundred and fifty-five is *cinque cento cinquanta cinque.* A writer from a local magazine interviews me at the corner bar and I try to answer a couple questions in Italian but quickly stumble, lost in the maze after two steps. A fictional story, in Italian, is a *racconto,* which has a root in common with our English word *account.* But an account, as in a "record," translates as *narrazione. Storia* is history. A novel is a *romanzo* and a historical novel is a *romanzo storico.* Romance, as a literary genre, is *romanzo* or *racconto.*

In the Dutch, French, and German editions of my last book, the word *roman* appears under the title: a novel. But in Italian, a *romano,* is, of course, a person from Rome. At least, I assume, *novella,* in Italian, has to mean "novella" in English, but it can also mean fiction in general, or, to make matters more confusing, a short story. It also means "new," or "news." Augh.

I try to tell the interviewer I have just finished a short story and am trying to resuscitate a half-drafted historical novel, but he ends up explaining the difference between a *resoconto* and a *racconto.*

Pelé, I tell him, left for Peru a paratrooper, but perished as puree.

Beneath the city that is the Italian language there are huge underground cities, Italo-Dalmatian, Tuscan, Latin, Greek, and beneath them catacombs of Oscan and Umbrian and Sabine, lightless tunnels opening to caverns, ghosts and bones, crypts opening to still deeper, fainter tunnels, the echoes of sentences in tribal languages that never had an alphabet in which to write them down. Slumbering tunnels of cuneiform, aquifers of hieroglyphics, razor-thin channels rising from Kurgan to Greek, Greek to Latin, Latin to Italian—the history of the world is compressed invisibly inside the words we say to each other, in whatever language—*mother, madre, mater, mētēr*—the sounds Henry and Owen are right now trying to fit their mouths around.

On the first of July, we wake to thunder. It cracks over the city twice, three times. The windows tremble in their frames. We stand in the terrace doorway and watch lightning split the darkness. After a minute or so, the spotlighted flank of the Vittoriano vanishes. A second later the rest of the city goes black. Our electricity goes, the clocks winking out, the fans spinning down. The trees across the street have plunged into shadow, as if a heavy carpet has unfurled over the city.

There's a distant crackle, like static. Then a pause, an inhalation, the only sound a fading engine, the last running motor on earth, maybe, and the air above the street goes from black to white.

It rains so hard we cannot see past the terrace railing. Water catapults down the windows. Soon the wind is forcing water across the sills and Shauna is grabbing towels from the bathroom. The boys wake and bury their foreheads into our shoulders but don't cry. "It's only rain," Shauna tells them. "Only rain." For a few minutes we hold them in the kitchen. The building roars. Hail pounds the terrace.

As quickly as it came, it passes. The trees drip and the street steams, furrows of hail glimmering palely in the gutters, and the Vittoriano reemerges, glowing down in the city. We set our sons back in their cribs. The fans start back up. Shauna hangs the wet towels over the shower rod. A *motorino* cruises past in the street. In the gaps between clouds, stars burn.

A few days after the storm, we roll Henry and Owen to the Pantheon, and—for the first time in that big, crowded space—let them out of the stroller. They rattle the fencing around some renovation scaffolding, they wander in a forest of legs. Owen crouches at the divisions of colors in the marble floor—ivory gives to red, red gives to gray—and slaps his hands on the stone and plays his stomping game in the circles and squares, standing and looking at us and grinning and bouncing in his little sandals.

We chase after them. The love for your kids, I'm learning, is a kind of love that has no conclusion, a feeling that multiplies back on itself. It's unquantifiable and almost certainly inexhaustible: No matter how many children you had, no matter what your children did, could you ever run out of that love?

If there is a God, His devotion to us is like that, like the way we feel about our children. And it feels as if something in the Pantheon expresses that, in the intersection of structure and sky, in the simultaneous expression of a building renewed and a building in ruin, the way the circle of light at the top lingers when everything else is in darkness.

Through the oculus, against a roiling backdrop of cloud, a single gull floats past, white and tiny, high above the city. I blink; in the intertwining heat and dust around me I see the heads of believers two thousand years gone, their faces turned up. Sons, daughters, mothers, fathers.

At noon in a Roman July, the sun is tiny, a blinding thumbtack pinned into the blue, but it fries us like ants on the cobbles. The city has become a series of superheated corridors. Girls tug off their stockings and soak their calves in fountains; monks and nuns walk about in their heavy outfits like refugees from another century.

Today is another holiday—I don't even have the energy to find out what this one is. Tiers of undergarments hang stock-still on clotheslines; the shops are closed. Piazza Garibaldi is lined with men sitting in parked cars reading newspapers. The boys are sweat-drenched in their stroller, chugging milk, hair plastered to their scalps.

In a few weeks, by mid-August, practically all the Romans will have abandoned their city to the tourists, *ferragosto,* and the stores will close and the piazzas will bake. We'll be gone, too.

When we get back to the apartment, I drag empty duffel bags out from beneath the bed and shake them out the windows. Owen and Henry climb into one and giggle. Clumps of dust drift through the bedroom.

"Soon we're going home," Shauna tells them, and Owen latches on to the word somehow and starts chanting, "Homehomehome," until it becomes indistinguishable from his word for *more.*

"Mo, mo, mo," sings Owen. "Mo, mo, mo," sings Henry.

In the Tom Andrews Studio I pull down the photos of B-17s and bombed-out cities. I fold the pages of my novel into manila folders. I'll finish it in Idaho, I tell myself, although I might be lying.

I spend the rest of the morning reading the last volume of Pliny's *Natural History.* "In the whole world," he writes, "wherever the vault of heaven turns, Italy is the most beautiful of all lands, endowed with all that wins Nature's crown. Italy is the ruler and second mother of the world—with her men and women, her generals and soldiers, her slaves, her outstanding position in arts and crafts, her abundance of brilliant talent, her geographical location and healthy, temperate climate, her easy accessibility for all other peoples, and her shores with their many harbors and kindly winds that blow towards her."

Out in the garden, heat gilds the pathways, the walls. The canopies of the pines stand on their thin trunks, motionless, dizzy. Pliny is wrong, I think. Every place has its own beauty. In Detroit, Michigan, I once got caught in a blizzard on the interstate, ice piling up on the wipers, the taillights in front of me inching along. At one point the wind suddenly died and the snowfall seemed to pause for a second in midair, tens of thousands of individual crystals, a field of diamonds suspended above the windshield. Then it began to blow *up*—a blizzard in slow-motion reverse. In Nairobi, Kenya, above an impossibly crowded market, the odors of clay and bodies and sewage all around, I watched a woman unfurl a banner above a stall, and the wind tore it from her hands and it opened and flapped in front of the sun, light saturating silk, before blowing out across the rooftops.

The world is not a pageant: beauty is as unquantifiable as love. Geography is not something that can be ranked.

The *Natural History,* the umbrella pines, Borromini's Sant'Ivo, the question of the starlings, and the question of fatherhood—my interest in them all rotates around one question: If we creatures are on earth only to extend the survival of our species, if nature only concerns itself with reproduction, if we are supposed to raise our kids to breeding age and then wither and slide toward death, then why does the world bother to be so astoundingly, intricately, breathtakingly beautiful? Is it all merely genetic variation? Geology and weather? Chemical twitch, electrical impulse, feathers and mating calls?

Pliny can't answer. I return the *Natural History* to the library downstairs. I clean the Tom Andrews Studio and carry my things out through the courtyard, down the front steps, past the circular entrance fountain in the gravel. A blackbird lands on the fountain's lip, not ten feet from me, hops forward, and begins to drink. It closes one yellow-rimmed eye. Then it vanishes.

Marco and his wife, Lula, come over. She has had the twins; they are three months old now, and spending the afternoon with her mother in Trastevere. Both parents look exhausted, gray in their cheeks, swipes of violet beneath their eyes. They hold hands, smile. It as if Shauna and I are looking in a mirror, gazing at former versions of ourselves.

Marco marvels at our terrace; "*Lula, la terrazza,*" he calls, and she and Shauna walk out to join us. Henry and Owen run laps around their little pool. We stand in the heat and drink Fanta and stumble through half English, half Italian: nap schedules, diaper brands, breast-feeding—we are soldiers from different armies fighting similar wars.

"If you can," Shauna says, "get them on the same nap schedule. *Insieme?* Together? Otherwise you will have no time for yourself."

Lula nods.

"It's hard," Shauna says, and she and Lula share a look. It is strange to think that we are suddenly the experienced ones, we who knew nothing about raising babies a year ago.

Before Marco and Lula leave, we pile hand-me-downs into their hatchback: sacks of baby clothes, crib sheets, a rug, a bucket of oversize LEGOs. They are grateful but not with the effusiveness that Americans might be; they seem to take it as a matter of course—what else would we do with this stuff?

A few hours later, we say good-bye to Laura and her family, who are going to spend the next month riding trains from Rome all the way up to Lapland. *"A presto,"* I tell Laura, though they'll return from Finland to Massachusetts and I'm not so sure we'll see them soon.

Five days before we leave Italy, we take the boys overnight to a little Umbrian hill town called Spello. We pile onto the train: two babies, two strollers, two duffel bags, two baby-carrying backpacks, two liters of milk, each carton so damp from humidity that it feels, pouring them, as if my thumb might punch through the cardboard.

Before the train has even departed Termini, Henry and Owen have become bored with the seat-belt clasps, the electric window shades, and the flip-up ashtray lids. They squirm in our arms and stomp our groins with their little sandals. Every toy or book we present is promptly tossed to the floor. By Tiburtina, ten minutes out, they are sprinting up and down the aisles, smacking their heads into armrests.

"You know how you're sitting on an airplane," Shauna says, "and some haggard people start down the aisle with a bag in one hand and a screaming baby in the other, and all you can think is 'Please don't be in the seat next to me, please don't be in the seat next to me'?"

"Yes."

"We *are* those people now."

Spello boils with red and pink geraniums. We push the boys up the streets in their stroller and eat ice-cream bars and let them stagger around a dusty playground in the heat. Villagers smile at us; the sun swings low across the vineyards. In the evening we eat pizza and turn down the thermostat in our hotel room to a temperature only American consciences would allow.

At 3 a.m. the full moon stares like an eye through the window. Owen is crying in his Portacrib. I close the drapes; I rub his back. For the next half hour I rock him in the bathroom. The moon, even through the curtains, is so bright you'd think it must have its own heat.

In Rome yesterday, as I waited in line at the self-service train-ticket machine, a woman with mud in her hair and three swipes of dirt across her cheek accosted the man in front of me. He refused to give her any money, and she was cursing and shuffling her feet, and I could see some last thread of self-control give way inside her, like a rusty wire, and she closed her eyes and opened them and punched the man in the sternum. He staggered and almost fell. I was extending a tentative arm when she threw her oversize bottle of beer at him. Amazingly, it didn't break. It bounced off his leg and rang on the floor, and the three of us watched it roll, turning over a couple of times before coming to a rest, a couple swallows of beer still inside.

Hostility, fervency—these hill towns have walls around them for a reason. Hannibal and his Carthaginians murdered legionnaires in the hills above Tuoro twenty-two hundred years ago, and after that there were the Guelfs, the Lombards, the duchy of Spoleto, the pope tyrants, all the rawboned, hopelessly cruel noble families of the early Renaissance, and all the strangers who wandered between towns with nothing to lose. Photos of Tuscany and Umbria and their sunflowers and lonesome cypresses and brown-shuttered villages are plastered in tourist offices all over Italy, and the promise is peace—seasoned pork, sunshine, romance, vines and olives, frescoes and festivals. But the history of violence is in the stones. Foligno, just five kilometers from us, was bombed into nothingness sixty years ago. Mignano, San Pietro, San Vittore—all of them were wiped out during the war. Cassino isn't that far away, either, where Germans and Americans and New Zealanders and Poles (the grandfathers of tourists sleeping in the rooms around us) died in droves on the rocks below the old monastery.

What has Italy taught me? Not to count on too much. Any minute a trio of jets will come screaming over the apartment or a diaper will mysteriously disintegrate or a baby will skip his naps. Transportation workers strike at will. A beggar's tin can lurches from nowhere. Count on sun and it rains.

Look closely and the picturesque inevitably cracks apart and becomes more interesting. In our little hotel room I sit on the closed lid of the toilet, Owen's head on my shoulder. Sometimes his scalp smells like wet, uncooked rice. Once, damp leaves. Tonight it smells like a deep, cold lake in summer.

The town sleeps; his little heart beats against mine.

Three days before we leave, Rome gives us one cool night. I sleep more deeply than I have since the boys were born. In a dream I am standing in an umbrella pine like the one outside the Tom Andrews Studio except that I somehow am the tree: I feel the wind in the needles as I might feel wind in the hairs on my arms. When I turn, the tree turns. Henry and Owen approach and stand beneath my trunk and open their coats and little white birds flutter out. I reach down: they—the birds and the boys—climb up into me. We look out at an endless white city, silver domes shining between temples, slices of light dropping through the clouds, flotillas of swans like white dots on liquid-metal ponds.

At noon Shauna and I sit in the garden eating mozzarella, tomato, and vinegar sandwiches. The breeze is mild. The boys stagger beneath the trees nearby and pick up fallen apricots and occasionally bite into one. We have an entire conversation and still the boys are fine—they don't need anything, don't need us chasing after them, don't require milk or consolation. It is perhaps the first time that we've been able to talk to each other for fifteen minutes, while the boys are awake, without having to pay a babysitter for the privilege.

A limitless sense of well-being comes washing over me, big creamy clouds riding through the sky, leaves fluttering softly. A year is an infinity of perceptions: not just the shapes of starlings and the death of the pope and watching our sons learn to walk, but the smell of roasting meat in an alley, the dark brown eyes of a beggar on a church step, a single dandelion seed settling soundlessly onto the habit of a nun who is riding the tram. This year has been composed of a trillion such moments; they flood the memory, spill over the edges of journal entries. What is it physicists tell us? Even in a finite volume, there are an infinite number of points.

But today, in the cool grass, the experience feels whole and unified and sweet. It feels as if a prism has slowly been turned, and the world has gradually come back into alignment. The edges of the clouds are seemingly sharper against the blue than they've ever been in the history of the world.

At dawn, on the morning after Henry and Owen were born, I left the hospital and rode my bicycle back to our apartment through the slush and climbed onto the porch and got our mail—which included the envelope that would send us to Rome—and carried it inside. I remember that as I passed through the door, I was amazed to find the material objects of our former life still intact—a magazine facedown on the couch and a vase of store-bought daisies on the table and photos of nieces taped to the refrigerator. Everything was exactly as we had left it twentysome hours before. I had assumed, during the night, Owen crying in his mother's arms, Henry in intensive care, nurses orbiting quietly around him, machines chiming behind curtains, that *everything* would have changed, that our old lives would have been destroyed and nothing could ever be the same again. But here were my books and computer and e-mail waiting to be answered and the same brown carpet on the stairs and our hamper of laundry and the two new Moses baskets, still in plastic bags, waiting for their occupants to come home.

There was our old life, in the apartment, in which we had time to finish most of the tasks we started and took long showers and remembered to water our plants. And there was our new life, in the hospital a mile away, in which Shauna needed morphine and two babies needed to eat every three hours around the clock and a tiny boy in a

Plexiglas incubator would need to be brought breast milk and given IVs and radiated with ultraviolet light.

I remember thinking, We're going to have to figure out how to combine our old life with our new life.

Over a year later, we still have days of mind-crushing fatigue, midnights when I think I'm pouring milk into a bottle but am actually pouring it all over the counter. Yesterday I spent five minutes trying to remember my parents' zip code.

But now there are mornings like this one, when we wake up and realize we've slept through the entire night, and we stroll though the gardens as if we are normal again, as if we are finally learning the syllables of this strange, new language.

In a poem Tom Andrews once asked the Lord to "afflict me with Attention Surplus Disorder so I can see what is in front of my face." I will try to always remember the eyes of the oldest Romans as they settled upon Henry and Owen in the stroller, that slow recognition, that wash of joy. More keenly than anyone, perhaps, they felt the transforming power of youth. They leaned forward on their canes. They wanted to be closer.

In a sense, this year, our predicament has been the same as Rome's: to reconcile the new life with the old life, to tunnel an exit back into the future.

I wish I'd gotten to know more Italians. I wish we'd invited Maria to dinner, the woman at the pasta shop who calls Henry *Enrico* and lifts him out of the stroller every time we come in and passes him around behind the counter, who loves to rent an RV in the summer and drive it north into

Switzerland, who is lovely but a bit crestfallen, too, not from any tragedy I know about but simply from the passage of time, pressing two fingers to her lips as she shows me a photo of her own son, now twelve or thirteen.

I wish I'd spent three or four days in the folds of the Alban Hills I can see from our terrace, tramping in the snow and drinking *colli albani* at tiny farmhouses and eating snails and looking back across the valley at the distant haze of the city. I wish I'd started one morning in Umbria with a sack full of sandwiches and a hired canoe and floated the Tiber all the way back to Rome and climbed out of the canoe and walked home. I wish I'd spent a night in Maremma, on the coast west of Florence, where there are supposed to be stands of umbrella pines beside the beach that stretch for miles.

I wish I'd asked a monk to let us into the catacombs beneath one of the churches on the Appian Way with only the stub of a candle, no flashlights, no bulbs in the ceilings, and let us wander through the ancient quarries down there in the blackness, the cool damp, the soft walls, underground avenues opening here and there, the thousand tombs scrolling past, and their little stone shelves on which sat glass vials of martyrs' blood, and only the one quivering flame to guide us.

I wish I'd found a way to get Pope John Paul II to have blessed Henry and Owen, their little faces turned up at him, his old, jeweled fingers quivering slightly, reaching out to brush their foreheads.

Two days before we leave, a family passing in front of the Academy asks me for directions to the Fontanone.

They are speaking Italian but have the look of tourists, slightly lost, sore-footed, rushing nowhere. Northerners perhaps.

"Follow me," I say. We descend, turn left: the chain-link fence, the roaring blue pool. At the railing, across from the fountain, they gasp as they lean into the view. The father burrows in a backpack and produces a camera. Far below us is the dark saucer of the Pantheon, the blue tourist balloon at the Villa Borghese, the Vittoriano, the clusters of rooftops: the city.

Water splashes behind; Rome twists below; clouds stream overhead.

"*Eccolo!*" the youngest girl says, and flourishes a hand. "*Ecco Roma!*"

Here is Rome.

Tacy comes to work for the last time. She has not yet found another job. "When I first came to Italy," she says, "I applied for some hotel jobs. Receptionist, concierge. The ads said they needed fluency in English. But when they called me into the office and looked at me, they didn't even want to hear me speak. They said, 'No, we are looking for applicants whose *first* language is English.'"

Sweet, beautiful Tacy: lately she has come into the apartment with bright green ivy leaves, big as sheets of paper, and let the boys run their fingers over them.

When it's time for her to go home, all three of us cry. Shauna stuffs cash and a thank-you card into Tacy's purse, as if this somehow absolves us of understanding how much more difficult her situation is than ours, as if a few hundred dollars will ease the work of replacing another under-the-table job, wiring money every week to the Philippines, eight thousand miles between her and her fourteen-year-old son, whose face she has not seen, whose hair she has not smelled, in almost three years.

We give her the blanket off our bed; we give her our extra dishes. I have to convince Shauna not to give her the remaining balance of our checking account.

I wait in the heat outside the butcher's stall for the last time. Three women are in line ahead of me. One, the oldest, turns and leans over the stroller.

"Sono gemellini?"

Yes. Little twins.

"Che belli," she says, and unleashes a torrent of Italian. I can follow very little. Something about the apartment adjacent to her own. Something about young children. She seems to be laying down several narrative strands, her fingers feeding yarn into an invisible loom. There are twins who are girls, there is a sports car, there is a phone call on Christmas Eve.

For a full minute her story builds. Words fly past me. I hear "flowers"; I hear "loaf of bread." But she is leaning in now; I am at the business end of her index finger, miles past the point where I might ask her to slow down.

The women in front of us depart with their purchases. The butcher slaps a veal loin onto his board, calls out, "Signora Cimorini?" Without slowing her story, she turns her index finger toward him, waggles it once, then tucks it away. Her story has begun to peak now, and behind the curved lenses of her glasses I see that she has begun to cry.

Abruptly she pauses. She chews her lip, caught in a whirlpool of memory.

"So beautiful," she says. "These girls."

I try, "On Christmas?"

This sets her nodding and crying harder. Tears fall one after another down her cheeks. The butcher calls her again. She looks up and blinks, and it takes her a few seconds to respond before telling him to make the meat thinner.

The boys watch her, drinking their milk.

"Santo Cielo," I finally say, good heavens, because it sometimes makes Italians smile. She pulls a handkerchief from her handbag and wipes her eyes. Should I hug her? I do nothing. I blink. The butcher is telling her that her veal will cost nine euros, and she pours a mess of coins onto the counter and he selects what she owes.

Before she leaves she kisses each of the boys good-bye.

One final morning. The sky is so blue it is almost black, the sun raining its hot light onto everything. I go to work in the Tom Andrews Studio one last time, a wave from Lorenzo in his little lodge, ankles crossed, eyes up at the television. The courtyard fountain splashes quietly; the jasmine holds a few last listless blooms.

The long upstairs hallway, the straight runner of red carpet, the white doors of fellows' apartments ticking past. The key. The door. The window, the rumpled cot, a broken pencil on the desk.

I open my journal. I look out at the trunk of the umbrella pine. In my mind, in my memory, I walk through Trastevere, cross the river downstream of Tiber

Island, and climb an overgrown pedestrian ramp called
the Clivo di Rocca Savella. I have climbed this ramp only
once before, but as I sit at my desk, my image of it is clear:
the green flowing over its walls, the water-stained brick,
the light bouncing off the stones. Buttresses line both
sides; the cobbles are furred with mosses.

At the top, the Aventine Hill is leafy and quiet; the
shutters of houses slip past. I take a right; soon the street
dead-ends into a piazza. On the northwest side, across
from the Egyptian consulate, a locked green door prevents entry into the gardens behind the priory of the
Knights of Malta. The paint is weathered, the bronze
hardware tarnished at the edges, anchored by four screws.
I press my eye to the keyhole.

Framed in the oval are two parallel lines of hedges,
interwoven at the top. Between is one of the most wonderful views in the world. The gaze soars over the Cir-
cus Maximus, skirts the Janiculum, and flies through a
mile of space. It comes to rest dead center on the dome
of St. Peter's. From here, through this keyhole, the vast
church, which struck Henry James "from the first as the
hugest thing conceivable," is nothing but a toy, a vaporous
dollhouse, its little pillars balanced atop a campanile in
the foreground, the lower half of the church obscured
behind a stand of pines like tiny flowers.

If only I could slip in the key and swing open the gate,
I could pluck up St. Peter's and balance the church in the
palm of my hand.

To be framed in hedges is the right thing; they frame
the cathedral in the way the countryside frames Rome,
Alban Hills on one side, Sabines on the other, fields and
apartment blocks and ruins spreading outside the walls,

the amber and purple and green of the distances, the blues of dusk, the swale of aqueducts and vineyards and olive groves that hem in Rome, girdling it, burying it.

Kingdom and time, architecture and weeds. Rome is huge; Rome is tiny.

A breeze sighs through the studio window, ruffling the pages of my notebook. My eye returns. The one continuous thing through Rome's history, from the Etruscans to Pliny to Caravaggio to Pope John Paul to Henry and Owen, is the light: the light at dawn, at sunset. The light tiptoes across everything, exposing it anew, whispering, Here is this! Here is this! *Ecco Roma!* Bursting out of the sun, streaking through space, skirting Venus, just over eight minutes old, but eternal, too, infinite—here comes the light, nameless and intangible, streaming 93 million unobstructed miles through the implacable black vacuum to break itself against a wall, a cornice, a column. It drenches, it crenellates, it textures. It throws the city into relief.

The coins fall through the slot; the illumination box clicks on.

When we eat a steak, we build its proteins into our bodies and become part cow. Eat an artichoke, become part artichoke. Drink a glass of orange juice, become part orange tree. Everything eventually corrupts: from our first draft of milk, we are corrupted, the world is corruption, time is corruption, and we are forever hungering for more.

I wonder if the same thing is true for this Roman light: If enough of it enters our eyes, if we look at something long enough, maybe we incorporate it. Maybe it becomes part of us. Maybe it flashes around inside us, endlessly reflecting, saturating everything.

The oculus of the Pantheon, the dome of St. Peter's, the tufted pillars of the umbrella pines, and the keyhole in the green door outside the gardens of the priory of the Knights of Malta on the Aventine Hill—they are all eyes of God. We look through them; they look through us. Everything is designed around the light.

Tomorrow we go home. Boise, for a while, anyway, will probably seem easy after this—all the addresses in English, all the street signs intelligible, all the supermarket vegetables waxy and uniform. Stores will be open when the posted hours say they'll be open, and weeks might pass without my needing to look at a map. When the boys get sick, we'll know where to take them and we won't have to dial two dozen numbers to talk to one of our friends.

Going home, I think, will be like waking up from a long and complicated dream, when you realize you are in your bedroom and everything around you is as it was but now slightly unfamiliar, and maybe slightly disappointing, too.

Rome has watched so many artists come and go, fixing its varying imprints on them, that I am hardly worth mentioning, hardly a blade of grass. It is Rome itself, and the idea of it—like the American Academy—that endures, beyond any of the individuals who pass through it. People dedicate themselves to it for a time, then the revolving arms of the seasons whisk them away. Rome is personless, almost immaterial. It is what exists between the buildings, beneath the lawns; it obliges its visitors to recognize what is hidden.

Look at the writers: Dante, Byron, Wharton, Calvino, D'Annunzio, Moravia, Pasolini. Goethe, who broke his celibacy here. Keats, who left his body here. Hawthorne, who saw his marble faun here. Charles Dickens, Henry James, Bernard Malamud. Saint Augustine. Ovid. Virgil. Horace. Cicero. Pliny the Elder. To see a list of even the ones who have worked in this same studio or the studios down the hall is to read off the spines on a serious bookshelf: William Styron, John Ciardi, Harold Brodkey, Anne Sexton. Ralph Ellison, who supposedly tried to cook pig's feet in the kitchen downstairs. Tom Andrews, whose forearms sweated into the wood of this very desk. Eleanor Clark, wife of Robert Penn Warren, who came to Rome on a fellowship to write a second novel but soon found the city had overwhelmed it. "It lasted there," she'd later say, "at most two weeks."

So many words spent in one place, on one place—who could have the nerve to slip even one more sentence into the pile?

I know nothing. I lived in Rome four seasons. I never made it through the gates between myself and the Italians. I cannot claim to have become, in even the smallest manner, Roman. And yet I can't stop myself: a pen, a notebook, the urge to circumscribe experience.

Roma, they say, *non basta una vita.* One life is not enough.

The Tiber threads beneath the bridges, another pope wakes and pulls on his alb, the summer heat climbs toward the meridian. The seasons make their circuit. Already the earth is tilting away from the sun; the nights are cooling. Soon enough the chimney swifts will leave for Africa and the elms will drop their leaves and snow will whiten the hills.

In the restaurants chefs prepare their gnocchi and cala-

mari and *bruschetta* and *straccetti*. At the market the vegetable ladies stack their apricots and pluck their zucchini
flowers. Shoppers tug their grocery carts and old men tap
their canes against the runnels and monks with white
faces and black cassocks whisper down pillared aisles and
beautiful women stride over cobbles in three-inch heels.
Tourists gaze up through the oculus of the Pantheon. Out
by the train station Tacy pads through her apartment,
knowing there is a good chance she won't see Henry and
Owen again for the rest of her life.

At dusk, between treetops, scraps of the city show
themselves like pieces of dreams, and tonight the streets
will throw the sun's heat back into the sky, soft pavements
and rooftop mirages, the reaching ivy, the swirling traffic,
the spinning fans, the tracking clouds, everything and
anything, the city of always.

I close my notebook. I start down the hallway, making
for home.

Notes

Epigraph   Pliny, *Natural History,* trans. H. Rackham (Cambridge, MA: Harvard University Press, 1942), bk. 2, chap. 38, 1:247.

14   *"The bark is gray-brown* Simon & Schuster's Guide to Trees (New York: Simon & Schuster, 1977), Plate 34.

15   *"Above all, it is fitting* The Log of Christopher Columbus, Robert H. Fuson, ed., trans. (Camden, ME: International Marine Publishing Company, 1987). Excerpts at http://www.saintjoe.edu/~ilicias/columbuslogentries.html.

29   *"Einstein slept ten hours* João Magueijo, *Faster Than the Speed of Light: The Story of a Scientific Speculation* (New York: Perseus Books, 2003), 31.

29   *"Two-thirds of 'great' male* Nicholas Wade, "Ideas & Trends; Prime Numbers: What Science and Crime Have in Common," *New York Times,* July 27, 2003.

31   *"Athletes when sluggish* Pliny, *Natural History,* trans. Rackham, bk. 8, chap. 42, 3:75.

31   *"Sexual intercourse cures* Pliny, *Natural History,* trans. John F. Healy (New York: Penguin Classics, 2004), bk. 28, p. 256.

34   *"natural gentleness toward* Pliny, *Natural History,* trans. Rackham, bk. 8, chap. 7, 3:19.

34   *"Where did Nature find* Ibid., bk. 8, 3: 433.

35   *In his world comets* Ibid., 3:503.

35 *cranes regularly assemble* Ibid., 3:415.

35 *moles tunneling* Ibid., 3:203.

36 *Lightning bolts make* Pliny, *Natural History,* trans. Healy, bk. 28, p. 259.

36 *dolphins "answer* Pliny, *Natural History,* trans. Rackham, bk. 9, chap. 7, 3:179.

36 *"Whales," he writes,* Ibid., 3:173.

37 *"In the long term, the clinical* Michael Breus, "Chronic Sleep Deprivation May Harm Health," http://www.webmd.com/content/article/64/72426.htm.

37 *"Different days pass verdict* Pliny, *Natural History,* trans. Rackham, bk. 7, chap. 40, 2:595.

38 *"Doerr's interest in nature* Neel Mukherjee, "Dream Lover," *New York Times,* November 7, 2004.

44 *"Headlands are laid open* Pliny, *Natural History,* trans. D. E. Eicholz (Cambridge, MA: Harvard University Press, 1942), bk. 36, chap. 1, 10:3–4

47 *"The dead drag a grappling hook* Tom Andrews, "Ars Poetica," in *Random Symmetries: The Collected Poems of Tom Andrews* (Oberlin, OH: Oberlin College Press, 2002): 84.

52 *In 1976, a doctoral student* From a letter to the magazine *New Scientist* 162, no. 2188 (May 29, 1999): 55.

58 *Three and a half million* Elin Schoen Brockman, "A Monument's Minder," *New York Times,* June 27, 2004.

61 *Pliny's writing, too,* Livy, *History of Rome,* bk. 1, chap. 36. "At all events," he writes, "auguries and the college of augurs were held in such honour that nothing was undertaken in peace or war without their sanction; the assembly of the curies, the assembly of the centuries, matters of the highest importance, were suspended or broken up if the omen of the birds was unfavourable." Translation: http://www.romansonline.com/Src_Frame.asp?DocID=Hor_LV01_36.

61 *Eagle-owls signified* Pliny, *Natural History,* trans. Rackham, bk. 10, chap. 14, 3:313.

62 *"supreme empire over the empire* Ibid., bk. 10, chap. 24, 3:323.

63 *Nero had a starling* Ibid., bk. 10, chap. 59, 3:369.

65 *Romans tossed newborns* Virgil, *Aeneid,* bk. 9. "Strong from the cradle, of a sturdy brood / We bear our newborn infants to the flood; / There bath'd amid the stream, our boys we hold / With winter harden'd, and inur'd to cold." That's Dryden's translation. Here's another: "To the streams we carry down our sons at birth / with harsh, frosty waves / we harden them."

68 *The bronze gilding* This is the same pope who, during the first days after his election, reputedly ordered that all the birds be killed outside his apartment windows because they disturbed his sleep.

81 *"As a protection against falling* Pliny the Younger, *The Letters of the Younger Pliny,* trans. Betty Radice (New York: Penguin Classics, 1969), 168.

87 *To spend a day* According to the World Health Organization, more than fifteen thousand people die in Italy every year because of car-exhaust fumes. http://www.italymag.co.uk/italy_regions/lazio_abruzzo/2005/current-affairs/rome-bans-cars-in-bid-to-cut-pollution/.

89 *This is the city where* Charles Dickens, *Pictures from Italy* (New York: Penguin Classics, 1998).

89 *the second-century senator and historian* Cassius Dio, *Roman History,* bk. 54, chap. 23. Available at: http://penelope.uchicago.edu/Thayer/E/Roman/Texts/Cassius_Dio/54*.html.

99 *"At this time many of the magistrates* Plutarch of Chaeronea, *Life of Julius Caesar,* trans. Robin Seager, chap. 61. Available at http://www.livius.org/caa-can/caesar/caesar_t18.html.

100 *After dark the carriages and crowds* Lots of them got trampled. In 1882, on the twenty-first of February, eleven horses killed fifteen onlookers in front of the church of St. Lorenzo in Lucina. Every year Jews were forced to pay a fee to avoid being forced to race each other on foot after the horses.

100 *"At a given signal* Goethe, *Italian Journey,* 445–76, http://www.romeartlover.it/Goethe.html.

100 *"The jingling of the [horses'] trappings* Dickens, *Pictures from Italy,* 122.

107 *"Notice how the masonry* In *Rome and a Villa,* Eleanor Clark quotes an early-twentieth-century architect who said much the same thing: "You see, the earlier you go, the better the workmanship."

109 *"a huge and shapeless tract* Tacitus, *Tacitus on Britain and Germany,* trans. H. Mattingly (New York: Penguin Classics, 1948), 52.

109 *The emperor Caligula's soldiers* Trevor Norton, *Underwater to Get out of the Rain* (Cambridge, MA: Da Capo Press, 2006), 25.

109 *"is as large as an eagle* Pliny, *Natural History,* trans. Rackham, bk. 10, chap. 2, 3:293.

109 *"could catch and gulp down birds* Ibid., bk. 8, chap. 14, 3:29.

109 *Scraping your gums with a tooth* Pliny, *Natural History,* trans. Healy, bk. 28, chap. 2, p. 252.

116 *"I heard his last breath* http://www.cnn.com/2005/WORLD/ europe/03/06/il.manifesto/.

123 *Nutella is a hazelnut-flavored* The average Italian family of four, the manufacturer's website says, consumes eight hundred grams of Nutella a year. That's 1.7 pounds.

124 *"Only he who always remembers* Pliny, *Natural History,* trans. Rackham, bk. 7, chap. 6, 2:535.

135 *"Whereas the signs of death are innumerable* Ibid., bk. 7, chap. 6, 2:535.

140 *In 1282, the Tuscan monk* Peter Pesic, *Sky in a Bottle* (Cambridge, MA: MIT Press, 2005), 26.

142 *"Though you are a whole world* Johann Wolfgang von Goethe, "Roman Elegies I."

148 *They couldn't draw an income* Even though their apartments are air-conditioned now, it is good for the cardinals that John Paul II did not die in August. In 1623, eight cardinals and forty of their assistants died of malaria during a sweltering nineteen-day conclave.

149 *"Look: it's splitting* Eleanor Clark, *Rome and a Villa* (South Royalton, VT: Steerforth Italia, 2000), 335.

169 *Media magnate Silvio Berlusconi's* Berlusconi's was indeed the longest in postwar Italy. In May 2006, after five years in power,

and weeks of controversy, he finally conceded defeat in parliamentary elections. "They will miss me," he reportedly told his ministers before handing in his resignation.

169 *"I'm not myself* Clark, *Rome and a Villa,* 314.

170 *"They are so strong* Pliny, *Natural History,* trans. Rackham, bk. 9, chap. 17, 3:195.

173 *At the end of the Empire* Clark, *Rome and a Villa,* 93.

185 *"In the whole world* Pliny, *Natural History,* trans. Healy, bk. 37, p. 376.

193 *"afflict me with Attention Surplus* Tom Andrews, "North of the Future," in *Random Symmetries* (Oberlin, OH: Oberlin College Press, 2002), 264.

198 *"from the first* Henry James, *Italian Hours* (New York: Penguin Classics, 1995), 134.

201 *"It lasted there* Clark, *Rome and a Villa,* xviii.

Acknowledgments

Heartfelt thanks to John Hartmann for allowing us to include a few of his marvelous sketches; to Rosecrans Baldwin and *The Morning News* (*www.themorningnews.org*) for conceiving, improving, and publishing my letters from Rome; to Becky Kraemer at Melville House Publishing, who convinced me my notebooks might be worth transforming into a book; to Laura Gratz-Piasecki and her family; to Steve and Jennifer Heuser; to Cristiano Urbani; to Sarah Kuehl and Ben Trautman for the help, friendship, and table; to *all* the fellows, especially Lisa Williams and George Stoll; to Azar Nafisi; to Lester Little and Lella Gandini, who presided over the Academy with singular grace; to Tacy, for everything; to my parents and brothers; to Hal and Jacque Eastman; to the incomparable Dana Prescott; to Lorenzo, Norm, G.P., and Pina; to the American Academy of Arts and Letters and the American Academy in Rome for giving writers such a breathtaking gift; to the Oberlin College Press for allowing me to reprint a few lines by Tom Andrews; to Emily Forland and Emma Patterson; to Anna deVries; to Clare Reihill for her warmth; to Nan Graham for her continued faith and confidence; to Wendy Weil for always understanding; and finally, of course, to Shauna, without whom the world is not the world, and Rome cannot be Rome.

If I got things wrong in here, and I'm sure I did, the fault is wholly my own.

The Shell Collector
by Anthony Doerr

'A show-stopping debut, as close to faultless as any
writer could wish for'
L. A. Times

'Unforgettable – not so much a book of short stories as a book of
short myths'
Elizabeth Gilbert (author of *Eat, Pray, Love*)

'I can think of very few authors who can put together a sentence
with such ecstasy, whose words sing with music and such sheer
rapture at what they embody'
The Times

A blind man spends his days roaming the beaches of Kenya
collecting shells, classifying them by feeling their whorls, spines and
folds in his fingers. A young woman discovers that she can explore
the inner world of an animal's mind by touching its freshly dead
body. A refugee from Liberia, who cannot escape the horrors that he
has witnessed, finds salvation in the clandesitne act of burying the
hearts of beached whales.

In *The Shell Collector* Antony Doerr illuminates both the
riotous dangers of the natural world and the rocky terrain of the
human heart.

About Grace
by Anthony Doerr

'Exceptional'
Daily Telegraph

'Unforgettable'
Guardian

'A stunning meditation on chance and pattern, exile and home.
Gorgeous, transporting and deeply, deeply satisfying'
Karen Joy Fowler (author of *We Are All Completely Beside Ourselves*)

David Winkler has lived on a remote Caribbean island for more
than two decades, after running away from his former life, his wife
Sandy and his daughter Grace.

David fell in love with Sandy at a supermarket in Alaska – as he
dreamt he would. Moving from Alaska to Ohio to escape his fear of
the future, they have a child: Grace. But a shadow of fear hangs over
David. And when the floods come, he can't face up to the future he
has seen for his little girl and leaves both the people he loves.

Twenty-five years later, he finally finds the strength to
discover his daughter's fate.

Memory Wall
by Anthony Doerr

'The stories in *Memory Wall* have such scope and depth that they hit
as hard as novels three times their length. Doerr has set a new
standard, I think, for what a story can do'
Dave Eggers

'Ambitiously wide-ranging and inventive, Doerr's six stories movingly
investigate the ways in which we are nothing without memory'
Sunday Times

'Doerr is a lusciously good stylist'
Guardian

A young boy in South Africa comes to possess an old woman's
secret, a piece of the past with the power to redeem a life. A teenaged
orphan moves from Kansas to Lithuania to live with her grandfather,
and discovers a world in which myth becomes real. A woman who
escaped the Holocaust is haunted by visions of her childhood
friends in Germany, yet finds solace in the tender ministrations
of her grandson.

Set on four continents, Anthony Doerr's collection of stories is about
memory: the source of meaning and coherence in our lives, the fragile
thread that connects us to ourselves and to others. The stories show
us how we figure the world, and show Anthony Doerr to be one of
the masters of the form.

All the Light We Cannot See
by Anthony Doerr

Sunday Times **Number One Bestseller**
New York Times **Number One Bestseller**
Winner of the Pulitzer Prize for Fiction 2015
Winner of the Andrew Carnegie Medal
for Excellence in Fiction 2015
Finalist for the National Book Award for Fiction 2014

A beautiful, stunningly ambitious novel about a blind French girl
and a German boy whose paths collide in Occupied France as both
try to survive the devastation of the Second World War.

For Marie-Laure, blind since the age of six, the world is full of mazes.
The miniature of a Paris neighbourhood, made by her father to teach
her the way home. The microscopic layers within the invaluable
diamond that her father guards in the Museum of Natural History.
The walled city by the sea, where father and daughter take refuge
when the Nazis invade Paris. And a future which draws her ever
closer to Werner, a German orphan, destined to labour in the mines
until a broken radio fills his life with possibility and brings him to
the notice of the Hitler Youth.

In this magnificent, deeply moving novel, the stories of
Marie-Laure and Werner illuminate the ways in which,
against all odds, people try to be good to one another.